107 Colon Cancer Salad and Meal Recipes:

Improve Your Nutrition Naturally to Prevent and Fight Cancer through Organic Superfoods

By

Joe Correa CSN

COPYRIGHT

© 2019 Live Stronger Faster Inc.

All rights reserved

Reproduction or translation of any part of this work beyond that permitted by section 107 or 108 of the 1976 United States Copyright Act without the permission of the copyright owner is unlawful.

This publication is designed to provide accurate and authoritative information in regard to the subject matter covered. It is sold with the understanding that neither the author nor the publisher is engaged in rendering medical advice. If medical advice or assistance is needed, consult with a doctor. This book is considered a guide and should not be used in any way detrimental to your health. Consult with a physician before starting this nutritional plan to make sure it's right for you.

ACKNOWLEDGEMENTS

This book is dedicated to my friends and family that have had mild or serious illnesses so that you may find a solution and make the necessary changes in your life.

107 Colon Cancer Salad and Meal Recipes:

Improve Your Nutrition Naturally to Prevent and Fight Cancer through Organic Superfoods

By

Joe Correa CSN

CONTENTS

Copyright

Acknowledgements

About The Author

Introduction

Commitment

107 Colon Cancer Salad and Meal Recipes: Improve Your Nutrition Naturally to Prevent and Fight Cancer through Organic Superfoods

Additional Titles from This Author

ABOUT THE AUTHOR

After years of Research, I honestly believe in the positive effects that proper nutrition can have over the body and mind. My knowledge and experience has helped me live healthier throughout the years and which I have shared with family and friends. The more you know about eating and drinking healthier, the sooner you will want to change your life and eating habits.

Nutrition is a key part in the process of being healthy and living longer so get started today. The first step is the most important and the most significant.

INTRODUCTION

107 Colon Cancer Salad and Meal Recipes: Improve Your Nutrition Naturally to Prevent and Fight Cancer through Organic Superfoods

By Joe Correa CSN

We still don't know what exactly causes colon cancer, but most doctors agree that a modern, Western diet high in fats and low in fibers increases the risk of this disease. These highly processed, unnatural, and unhealthy foods lead to chronic inflammatory diseases of the colon by affecting the microbes that live in it, which leads to cell degeneration. This is a good reason why you should focus more on eating healthy organic foods rather than jumping from one diet to another that often offer empty promises. Foods you have to include on a daily basis are: fresh fruits and vegetables, organic fish and poultry, nuts, seeds, and legumes. In order to clean your gastrointestinal tract and reduce the risk of colon cancer, your diet must be primarily based on beans, lentil, peas, and other foods that are high in folate. Along with valuable fiber, these foods are an enormous source of vitamin B that will protect your colon cells from damage.

When left untreated, harmless adenomatous polyps

transform into cancer which, just like all other types of cancers, can be a life-threatening condition. It is very important to identify colon cancer symptoms and prevent the disease from progressing.

There are also certain risk factors that may contribute to developing colon cancer. These factors include older age, inflammatory intestinal conditions, family history of colon cancer, sedentary lifestyle, poor diet, obesity, smoking, and alcohol.

Scientists agree that there is a strong connection between low-fiber, high-fat diet and colon cancer. Eating plenty of fresh fruit, vegetables, and fiber-rich whole grain will give your body an array of vitamins and minerals and play an important role in cancer prevention. However, making these small changes in your every day life can be a bit difficult due to busy schedules. For this reason, I have collected these powerful yet easy to prepare colon cancer preventing recipes. You will easily find all the ingredients in your local store and easily prepare a wonderful and healthy salad for the entire family in just minutes. These recipes are here to make your life better so get started right away!

COMMITMENT

In order to improve my condition, I *(your name)*, commit to eating more of these foods on a daily basis and to exercise at least 30 minutes daily:

- Berries (especially blueberries), peaches, cherries, apples, apricots, oranges, lemon juice, grapefruit, tangerines, mandarins, pears, etc.
- Broccoli, spinach, collard greens, sweet potatoes, avocado, artichoke, baby corn, carrots, celery, cauliflower, onions, etc.
- Whole grains, steel-cut oats, oatmeal, quinoa, barley, etc.
- Black beans, red bean beans, garbanzo beans, lentils, etc.
- Nuts and seeds including: walnuts, cashews, flaxseeds, sesame seeds, etc.
- Fish
- 8 – 10 glasses of water

Sign here

X_____

107 COLON CANCER SALAD AND MEAL RECIPES: IMPROVE YOUR NUTRITION NATURALLY TO PREVENT AND FIGHT CANCER THROUGH ORGANIC SUPERFOODS

1. Avocado Eggs with Greens

Ingredients:

1 avocado, halved and pitted

2 eggs

2 tbsp freshly squeezed lime juice

1 tsp dried thyme

½ tsp dried rosemary

¼ tsp red pepper flakes

¼ tsp sea salt

1 large tomato, chopped into chunks

1 cup lettuce, torn

1 cup baby spinach, chopped

1 cup arugula, chopped

Preparation:

Rinse lettuce, spinach, and arugula under cold running water and set aside to drain in a large colander.

Preheat the oven to 400 degrees. Line a small square baking pan with some parchment paper and set aside.

Cut avocado in half and remove the pit. Place avocado halves in a baking pan and brush with the lime juice. Slowly pour the eggs into each hole and sprinkle with thyme, rosemary, salt, and red pepper flakes.

Bake for 15 minutes or until set. Remove from the oven and cool for a while.

Meanwhile, in a large bowl, toss together tomato, lettuce, spinach, and arugula. Sprinkle with the remaining lime juice and serve with avocado.

Nutritional information per serving: Kcal: 205, Protein: 6.2g, Carbs: 12.4g, Fats: 16.3g

2. Egg Salad with Spinach and Nuts

Ingredients:

1 lb fresh spinach, torn

2 garlic cloves, crushed

½ tsp sea salt

2 eggs, hard-boiled

5 almonds, finely chopped

5 walnuts, finely chopped

¼ tsp chili flakes

Olive oil for the pan

Preparation:

Gently place eggs in a pot of boiling water. Cook for 10-12 minutes. Remove from the heat and drain. Cool to a room temperature and peel. Using a sharp knife, cut eggs in half. Set aside.

Now grease a large non-stick skillet with some olive oil and heat up over medium-high heat. Add garlic and stir-fry for two minutes. Add spinach and continue to cook for five minutes, stirring constantly. Season with chili flakes, give it a good stir and remove from the heat. Transfer to a serving plate and sprinkle with sea salt, chopped almonds, and walnuts.

Serve with boiled eggs. Optionally, add ½ cup of avocado chunks!

Nutritional information per serving: Kcal: 185, Protein: 14.7g, Carbs: 11g, Fats: 11.4g

3. Turkey Breast Salad

Ingredients:

8 oz boneless and skinless turkey breast, sliced into 1-inch thick slices

2 cups arugula

2 tbsp goat's cheese

5 almonds

5 walnuts

2 tbsp red wine vinegar

1 tbsp dried thyme

1 tomato, sliced

Preparation:

Remove the breast from the refrigerator about 30 minutes before use. Cover and let them it at the room temperature.

Preheat a non-stick grill pan to medium-high. Brush with some olive oil and add sliced turkey. Cook for 7-8 minutes or until lightly charred, turning halfway through.

Remove from the heat and cool for about five minutes while you assemble the salad.

In a small bowl, whisk together red wine vinegar, dried thyme, and olive oil. Set aside.

In a large bowl, combine together arugula, tomato, goat's cheese, almonds, and walnuts. Top with turkey breast and drizzle with the red wine mixture.

Serve immediately.

Nutritional information per serving: Kcal: 277, Protein: 28g, Carbs: 9.4g, Fats: 14.2g

4. Garlic Chicken and Vegetable Salad

Ingredients:

1lb chicken breast, sliced into half-inch thick slices

½ cup freshly squeezed lime juice

2 tbsp olive oil

½ cup parsley leaves, finely chopped

3 garlic cloves, crushed

1 tbsp cayenne pepper

1 tsp dried oregano

½ tsp sea salt

1 cup cherry tomatoes, sliced

1 cup arugula, chopped

1 cup lamb's lettuce, chopped

Preparation:

Rinse the meat under cold running water and drain in a large colander. Using a sharp knife, slice into approximately half-inch thick slices. Set aside.

In a medium bowl, combine olive oil with lime juice,

chopped parsley, crushed garlic, cayenne pepper, oregano, and salt.

Generously brush fillets with this mixture and cover. Refrigerate for 30 minutes.

Preheat a large, non-stick frying pan over medium-high heat. Remove the fillets from the marinade and pat-dry with a kitchen towel. Cook for 4-5 minutes on each side.

In a large bowl, combine together tomatoes, arugula, and lamb's lettuce. Add chicken and optionally, sprinkle with some lemon or lime juice.

Serve immediately.

Nutritional information per serving: Kcal: 283, Protein: 33.6g, Carbs: 6.2g, Fats: 13.7g

5. Chicken and Button Mushrooms Salad

Ingredients:

1lb chicken breast, cut into bite-sized pieces

3.5 oz button mushrooms, whole

1 medium-sized tomato, roughly chopped

2 oz lettuce

1 cucumber, sliced

1 tbsp olive oil

1 tbsp Dijon mustard

2 tbsp apple cider vinegar

1 tsp freshly squeezed lemon juice

1 tbsp dried rosemary

½ tsp pink Himalayan salt

Kalamata olives (optional for serving)

Cooking spray

Preparation:

Rinse the meat under cold running water and pat dry with

a kitchen towel. Place on a cutting board and chop into bite-sized pieces. Set aside. In a small bowl, combine Dijon mustard with olive oil, dried rosemary, apple cider, and salt. Stir well and brush the meat with this mixture. Wrap in aluminum foil and refrigerate for 30 minutes. Meanwhile, spray a large, non-stick skillet with some cooking spray. Add button mushrooms and cook for 10 minutes, stirring occasionally. Remove from the heat and cool to a room temperature. Wash and prepare the vegetables. Place in a serving bowl. Add mushrooms and stir well. Set aside. Preheat the oven to 350 degrees. Line some parchment paper over a baking pan and set aside.

Remove the meat from the refrigerator and transfer into a baking pan along with the marinade.

Cook for 35 minutes, turning once. When done, remove the meat from the oven and chill to a room temperature. Serve with vegetables.

Nutritional information per serving: Kcal: 254, Protein: 34.5g, Carbs: 8g, Fats: 9.2g

6. Tuna Salad

Ingredients:

1 cup tuna, canned in water

3 eggs, hard-boiled

1 cucumber, sliced

¼ cup walnuts

½ cup fresh goat's cheese

1 cup baby spinach, finely chopped

½ carrot, sliced

1 tbsp freshly squeezed lemon juice

½ tsp salt

Preparation:

Gently place eggs in the pot of boiling water. Cook for 12 minutes. Remove from the heat and drain. Chill to a room temperature and peel. Slice one egg in half and chop the remaining two. Place in a serving plate.

Add vegetables and season with salt. Drizzle with lemon juice and top with tuna and the remaining egg.

Serve immediately.

Nutritional information per serving: Kcal: 208, Protein: 19.4g, Carbs: 4.9g, Fats: 12.7g

7. Warm Quinoa with Nuts and Cranberries

Ingredients:

1 cup quinoa

3 tbsp hazelnuts, minced

½ cup fresh parsley

1 small onion, finely chopped

2 garlic cloves, crushed

¼ tsp salt

2 tbsp olive oil

1 cup button mushrooms, sliced

¼ cup cranberries

Preparation:

Grease a small skillet with some olive oil or cooking spray and heat up over medium-high heat. Add sliced mushrooms and cook for 6-7 minutes, stirring constantly. Remove from the heat and season with salt. Set aside.

Add quinoa to a small, heavy-bottomed pan and pour in one cup of water. Bring to a boil over medium heat and gently simmer until all the liquid has evaporated. Stir occasionally.

When done, remove from the heat and cool for a while.

In a small bowl, combine together hazelnuts, parsley, salt, and one tablespoon of olive oil. Mix all well and add chopped onions and crushed garlic. Let it sit for 5-10 minutes.

Stir in cooked quinoa and mushrooms. Top with cranberries and mix well to combine. Serve immediately.

Nutritional information per serving: Kcal: 206, Protein: 6.1g, Carbs: 25.3g, Fats: 9.5g

8. Cucumber and Parsley Salad with Lime

Ingredients:

1 large cucumber, thinly sliced

2 garlic cloves, crushed

¼ cup fresh parsley, chopped

1 tbsp fresh lime juice

2 tbsp extra virgin olive oil

Salt and pepper to taste

Preparation:

In a small bowl, combine together garlic, lime juice, olive oil, and some salt and pepper. Mix all well and let it sit for 10 minutes. Meanwhile, peel and thinly slice cucumber. Transfer to a bowl and sprinkle with freshly chopped parsley. Drizzle with the garlic oil and optionally season with some more salt or pepper to taste. Refrigerate for at least 30 minutes before serving.

Nutritional information per serving: Kcal: 299, Protein: 2.8g, Carbs: 13.9g, Fats: 28.5g

9. Brown Rice Salad

Ingredients:

1 cup brown rice

3 spring onions, finely chopped

½ cup corn

1 red bell pepper, cut into strips

¼ cup fresh mint, finely chopped

2 tbsp extra virgin olive oil

1 tbsp apple cider vinegar

Salt to taste

Preparation:

Add rice in a medium saucepan and pour in two cups of cold water. Cover with the lid and bring to a boil over medium heat. Reduce the heat to low and cover with the lid. Cook over low heat for 15-18 minutes, stirring occasoanlly.

When done, turn off the heat and let the rice sit covered for another 10-15 minutes.

Meanwhile, drain corn in a small sieve and transfer to a

serving bowl. Prepare the vegetables. Cut pepper in half and remove stem and seeds. Cut into strips and add to a bowl. Finely chop onions and toss with corn and pepper.

Finally, add rice and stir in mint. Sprinkle with olive oil, apple cider vinegar, and some salt to taste.

Mix all well and serve.

Nutritional information per serving: Kcal: 353, Protein: 6.5g, Carbs: 57.9g, Fats: 11.5g

10. Fresh Vegetable Salad

Ingredients:

2 cups lettuce, torn

1 purple onion, diced

1 medium tomato, chopped

1 green bell pepper, diced

1 small chili, diced

1 cup baby spinach, chopped

2 tbsp extra virgin olive oil

1 tbsp apple cider vinegar

1 tsp fresh rosemary, finely chopped

¼ tsp salt

Preparation:

Add lettuce and baby spinach to a large colander and rinse thoroughly under cold running water. Set aside to drain.

Now, prepare the vegetables. Rinse tomato and pat dry with a kitchen towel. Chop into bite-sized pieces and add to serving bowl.

Cut green pepper in half and remove the seeds. Using a sharp knife, dice the pepepr and transfer to a bowl.

Dice onion and one small chili. Add all to a bowl and top with drained greens. Sprinkle with olive oil, apple cider vinegar, rosemary, and salt.

Mix all well and serve immediately.

Nutritional information per serving: Kcal: 196, Protein: 2.9g, Carbs: 15.6g, Fats: 15g

11. Sweet Carrot Salad

Ingredients:

1 medium-sized carrot, sliced

2oz baby spinach

1 medium-sized tomato, finely chopped

2oz rice spaghetti, soaked

1 small cucumber, finely chopped

¼ cup fresh blueberries

¼ cup honey

¼ cup fresh lime juice

1 tsp Dijon mustard

¼ tbsp ground cumin

Preparation:

Place the rice spaghetti in a deep pot and pour water enough to cover. Soak the rice spaghetti in water for about 15 minutes. Drain and transfer to a bowl. Set aside.

Rinse the spinach under running water and drain. Chop into small pieces and set aside.

Wash the tomato and chop into small pieces. Set aside.

In a large salad bowl, add chopped spinach, tomato, sliced carrot, and blueberries. Toss to combine.

In a small mixing bowl, combine honey, lime juice, Dijon mustard, and cumin. Mix until combined and drizzle over salad. Toss to combine and serve immediately.

Enjoy!

Nutritional information per serving: Kcal: 201, Protein: 3.4g, Carbs: 48.6g, Fats: 0.7g

12. Spring Salad with Black Olives

Ingredients:

5 cherry tomatoes

A handful of black olives

1 medium-sized onion, peeled and sliced

2 radishes, sliced

A handful of lamb's lettuce

2 tbsp freshly squeezed lime juice

3 tbsp extra virgin olive oil

Salt to taste

Preparation:

In a small mixing bowl, combine olive oil, lime juice, and salt. Mix until well combined and set aside.

Rinse the tomatoes and remove the stems. Cut into halves and set aside.

Wash the radishes and trim off the green parts. Cut into thin slices and set aside.

Rinse the lettuce using a large colander. Drain and chop

into small pieces.

In a large salad bowl, combine tomatoes, olives, onion, radishes, and lamb's lettuce. Drizzle with previously prepared dressing.

Toss to combine and serve immediately.

Nutritional information per serving: Kcal: 197, Protein: 2.7g, Carbs: 15.3g, Fats: 15.7g

13. Crispy Beans Salad with Lime Dressing

Ingredients:

½ red onion, peeled and sliced

2 oz green beans, cooked

3 cherry tomatoes, halved

1 red bell pepper, chopped

¼ cup fresh lime juice

3 tbsp olive oil

1 tsp honey

½ small shallot, minced

1 garlic clove, crushed

¼ tsp salt

Preparation:

Combine the lime juice with honey. Mix well with a fork. Slowly add the olive oil, whisking constantly. Now add the minced shallot, crushed garlic clove, and salt. Set aside.

Rinse the tomatoes and remove the stems. Cut into bite-sized pieces and set aside.

Cut the bell pepper lengthwise in half. Remove the stem and seeds. Cut into bite-sized pieces and set aside.

Now, in a large salad bowl, combine onion, green beans, cherry tomatoes, and bell pepper. Drizzle with previously prepared dressing and toss to combine.

Serve immediately.

Nutritional information per serving: Kcal: 268, Protein: 3.2g, Carbs: 20.5g, Fats: 21.6g

14. Lentil Salad

Ingredients:

1 cup lentils, cooked

1 medium-sized red bell pepper

½ cup sweet corn, drained

A handful of purple cabbage, shredded

A handful of lettuce, shredded

½ tsp salt

¼ tsp black pepper, freshly ground

2 tbsp olive oil

1 tbsp sesame seeds

Preparation:

First you have to cook your lentils. Use 3 cups of water for 1 cup of dry lentils. Cooked lentils will double in size. Bring the water to a boiling point, reduce the heat to medium and cover. Cook for about 15-20 minutes. Remove from the heat and drain. Transfer to a bowl and set aside.

Wash the pepper and cut lengthwise in half. Remove the stem and seeds. Chop into small pieces and set aside.

In a large colander, combine purple cabbage and lettuce. Rinse under running water and drain. Shred into tiny strips and set aside.

In a small mixing bowl, combine olive oil, sesame seeds, salt, and pepper. Mix until combined and set aside.

In a large salad bowl, combine cooked lentils, bell pepper, corn, cabbage, and lettuce. Drizzle with previously prepared dressing and toss to combine.

Serve immediately.

Nutritional information per serving: Kcal: 367, Protein: 18.7g, Carbs: 49g, Fats: 12g

15. Green Bean Salad

Ingredients:

1 lb fresh green beans

¼ cup extra virgin olive oil

2 garlic cloves, crushed

1 tbsp lime juice

Preparation:

Pour 4 cups of water in a deep pot. Bring to a boil over medium-high heat. Add beans and sprinkle with some salt. Cook for 5 minutes, or until tender. Remove from the heat and drain well. Transfer to a large bowl and let it chill for a while.

In a small mixing bowl, combine olive oil, garlic, and lime juice. Mix until well combined.

Drizzle the dressing over the beans and toss to coat well. Optionally, add a few lemon slices and finely chopped parsley for decoration before serving.

Nutritional information per serving: Kcal: 296, Protein: 4.4g, Carbs: 19g, Fats: 25.5g

16. Raspberry Salad with Pumpkin Seeds

Ingredients:

1 tbsp pumpkin seeds

2 cups fresh raspberries

¼ tsp fresh rosemary, finely chopped

2 tbsp fresh lime juice

1 tsp cumin powder

1 tsp agave syrup

1 cup lettuce, chopped

Preparation:

Place the raspberries in a large colander and rinse under running water. Drain and set aside.

Rinse the lettuce under running water and drain. Chop into small pieces and set aside.

In a small mixing bowl, combine lime juice, cumin powder, and agave syrup. Mix until well combined.

In a large salad bowl, combine lettuce and raspberries. Drizzle with previously prepared dressing and toss to combine.

Refrigerate for 20 minutes before serving.

Nutritional information per serving: Kcal: 234, Protein: 6.1g, Carbs: 46.7g, Fats: 6.2g

17. Broccoli Salad with Tomatoes

Ingredients:

2 cups broccoli, halved

2 large tomatoes, chopped

2 tbsp olive oil

1 tbsp dried parsley, ground

¼ tsp Italian seasoning

Salt and pepper to taste

1 tbsp lemon juice, freshly squeezed

Preparation:

In a small bowl, combine olive oil, dried parsley, Italian seasoning, salt, pepper, and lemon juice. Mix until well combined and set aside.

Rinse the broccoli and cut each in half. Set aside.

Pour 3 cups of water in a deep pot. Bring to a boil over medium-high heat. Add broccoli and cook for 20 minutes, or until tender. Remove from the heat and drain. Set aside to chill for a while.

Wash the tomatoes and remove the stems. Chop into small

pieces and set aside.

In a large salad bowl, combine broccoli and tomatoes. Drizzle with previously prepared dressing and toss to combine.

Serve immediately.

Nutritional information per serving: Kcal: 188, Protein: 4.3g, Carbs: 13.5g, Fats: 14.9g

18. Seafood Salad

Ingredients:

1 small pack frozen mixed seafood

1 tbsp olive oil

1 small onion

1 cup cherry tomatoes

1 tsp chopped, dry rosemary

1 tbsp sweet corn

¼ tsp salt

1 tbsp freshly squeezed lemon juice

Preparation:

Preheat the olive oil in a saucepan over medium-high heat. Add seafood mix and cook for 10 minutes, crumbling the frozen mixture with a wooden spoon. Carefully add ¼ cup of water and continue to cook for 5 more minutes. Remove from the heat and allow it to cool.

Meanwhile prepare the remaining ingredients.

In a small mixing bowl, combine lemon juice, salt, and rosemary. Mix until combined and set aside.

Rinse the tomatoes under running water and remove the stems. Chop into small pieces and set aside.

In a large salad bowl, combine seafood mix, onion, and cherry tomatoes. Drizzle with previously prepared dressing and toss to combine.

Serve immediately.

Nutritional information per serving: Kcal: 208, Protein: 11.7g, Carbs: 22.7g, Fats: 8.7g

19. Dandelion Greens Salad

Ingredients:

2 cups fresh dandelion greens, roughly chopped

1 Roma tomato, finely chopped

½ cup fresh lemon juice

1 tbsp yellow mustard

Sea salt to taste

Preparation:

Place the dandelion greens in a large colander and rinse under running water. Drain and chop into small pieces. Set aside.

Wash the tomato and remove the stem. Cut into bite-sized pieces and set aside.

In a small mixing bowl, combine lemon juice, yellow mustard, and sea salt. Mix until salt has been disolved.

Now, place the greens in a salad bowl and drizzle with previously prepared dressing. Toss to combine and serve immediately.

Instead of dandelion greens, feel free to use baby arugula,

baby spinach, or some other leafy green vegetable.

Nutritional information per serving: Kcal: 90, Protein: 4.7g, Carbs: 13.9g, Fats: 2.4g

20. Veal Salad with Fresh Veggies

Ingredients:

1 lb veal cutlets

1 large tomato

1 large green bell pepper

½ cup cabbage, grated

2 tbsp olive oil

¼ tsp dried thyme, ground

¼ tsp dried parsley, ground

1 garlic clove, minced

Salt and pepper to taste

Preparation:

Rinse the meat under running water and pat dry with a kitchen paper. Transfer to a cutting board and cut into thin strips. Generously rub with salt, pepper, thyme, parsley, and olive oil. Set aside for 10 minutes.

Meanwhile, preheat the grill to medium-high. Grill for 3-5 minutes on each side. Remove from the heat and set aside to chill for a while.

Prepare the remaining vegetables.

Cut the pepper lengthwise in half. Remove the stem and seeds. Chop into thin strips and set aside.

Wash the tomato and remove the stem. Chop into small pieces and set aside.

Now, combine bell pepper, tomato, and cabbage in a salad bowl. Top with meat and sprinkle with some more salt and olive oil.

Nutritional information per serving: Kcal: 343, Protein: 35g, Carbs: 4.9g, Fats: 20.1g

21. Grilled Chicken Salad

Ingredients:

2 pieces chicken breast, boneless and skinless

¼ cup silken tofu, sliced

1 cup lamb's lettuce

1 cup cherry tomatoes

1 small zucchini, chopped

¼ tsp of red pepper, ground

2 tbsp olive oil

¼ tsp salt

Preparation:

Wash and pat dry the meat with some kitchen paper. Transfer to a cutting board and cut into bite-sized pieces. Brush with some salt and olive oil and set aside.

Peel and chop the zucchini into thin slices. Sprinkle with some salt and set aside.

Preheat the grill to a medium-high heat. Add chicken and zucchini. Grill the chicken 2-3 minutes per side. Grill the zucchini 1-2 minutes per side.

Now, grill tofu for 2 minutes per side.

Rinse the lamb's lettuce using a large colander. Drain and transfer to a large bowl. Add cherry tomatoes, tofu, zucchini, and red pepper. Mix all well and top with chicken.

Serve immediately.

Nutritional information per serving: Kcal: 286, Protein: 26.2g, Carbs: 7g, Fats: 17.4g

22. Lettuce Salad with Walnuts

Ingredients:

2 cups Iceberg lettuce, chopped

1 large orange, peeled and wedged

2 tbsp walnuts, roughly chopped

¼ cup dates, pitted and finely chopped

1 tbsp fresh lemon juice

1 tbsp olive oil

¼ tsp dried thyme, ground

Preparation:

Place the lettuce in a large colander. Rinse under running water and drain. Chop into small pieces and place in a large bowl. Set aside.

Peel the orange and divide into wedges. Cut each wedge in half and add to the bowl with lettuce.

In a small mixing bowl, combine lemon juice, olive oil, and thyme. Mix until well combined and drizzle over the salad.

Finally top with dates and walnuts.

Serve immediately.

Nutritional information per serving: Kcal: 224, Protein: 3.6g, Carbs: 30.2g, Fats: 12g

23. Homemade Tuna Salad

Ingredients:

1 (12oz) tuna steak

¼ cup spring onions, chopped

2 tbsp extra-virgin olive oil

¼ tsp sea salt

¼ tsp chili pepper

1/8 tsp white pepper, ground

1 tbsp fresh lemon juice

Preparation:

Rinse the tuna steak under running water and pat-dry with a kitchen towel. Generously rub with salt, pepper, and olive oil. Set aside.

Meanwhile, preheat the grill to medium-high heat. Cook for 4-5 minutes on each side. Remove from the grill and set aside to chill for a while.

Using two forks, flake the tuna into thin strips. Transfer to a salad bowl, and add spring onions. Add the remaining olive oil and sprinkle with some salt.

Finally, drizzle with lemon juice and serve immediately.

Enjoy!

Nutritional information per serving: Kcal: 293, Protein: 34.1g, Carbs: 0.8g, Fats: 16.5g

24. Lettuce and Tomato Salad

Ingredients:

2 cups cherry tomatoes, roughly chopped

2 cups Iceberg lettuce, finely chopped

1 tsp apple cider vinegar

¼ tsp of sea salt

¼ tsp red pepper flakes

½ tbsp extra virgin olive oil

Preparation:

Rinse the cherry tomatoes and remove the stems. Roughly chop it into bite-sized pieces and set aside.

Using a large colander, rinse the lettuce thoroughly under running water. Drain and chop into small pieces. Set aside.

In a small mixing bowl, combine apple cider vinegar, sea salt, red pepper, and olive oil. Mix until combined and set aside.

Now, in a large salad bowl, combine cherry tomatoes and lettuce. Drizzle with previously prepared dressing and toss to combine.

Serve immediately.

Nutritional information per serving: Kcal: 142, Protein: 3.7g, Carbs: 17.6g, Fats: 8g

25. Creamy Chicken Salad

Ingredients:

4 oz chicken breast, skinless and boneless

1 cup Romaine lettuce, chopped

1 medium onion, peeled and sliced

5 cherry tomatoes, chopped

2 tbsp low-fat cream

1 tsp fresh parsley, finely chopped

1 tbsp extra-virgin olive oil

¼ tsp chili powder

1 tbsp lemon juice

Salt and pepper

Preparation:

Rinse the chicken under running water and pat-dry with a kitchen paper. Transfer to a cutting board and cut into thin slices. Using your hands, rub with some salt and pepper. Set aside.

In a small saucepan, combine cream, parsley, chili powder,

and a pinch of salt and pepper. Heat up over medium-high heat. Bring it to a boil and remove from the heat. Give it a good stir and set aside.

Preheat the grill to medium-high heat. Add chicken and cook for 3 minutes on each side. Remove from the grill and set aside.

Wash and prepare the remaining vegetables.

In a large salad bowl, combine lettuce, onion, and tomatoes. Top with chicken and drizzle all with cream sauce. Mix until well coated and serve immediately.

Enjoy!

Nutritional information per serving: Kcal: 223, Protein: 17.7g, Carbs: 19.2g, Fats: 9.5g

26. Leafy Greens Salad with Orange Dressing

Ingredients:

2 cups Iceberg lettuce, roughly chopped

1 cup baby spinach, roughly chopped

½ cup Mozzarella cheese, sliced

2 tbsp orange juice, freshly squeezed

1 tsp apple cider vinegar

½ tsp Italian seasoning

¼ tsp black pepper, ground

¼ tsp salt

Preparation:

In a large colander, combine lettuce and spinach. Rinse under running water and drain. Chop into bite-sized pieces and transfer to a large salad bowl. Set aside.

In a small mixing bowl, combine orange juice, apple cider vinegar, Italian seasoning, black pepper, and salt. Mix until well combined.

Cut the cheese into thin slices and add to the salad. Drizzle all with previously prepared dressing and toss to combine.

Optionally, add a few olives for some extra flavor.

Enjoy!

Nutritional information per serving: Kcal: 85, Protein: 5.6g, Carbs: 8.8g, Fats: 3.6g

27. Radicchio Salad

Ingredients:

1 large radish, roughly chopped

1 large cucumber, sliced

¼ cup lemon juice, freshly squeezed

1 tbsp fresh parsley, finely chopped

¼ tsp black pepper, ground

¼ tsp salt

1 tsp yellow mustard

Preparation:

In a small mixing bowl, combine lemon juice, parsley, pepper, salt, and mustard. Mix untill smooth and set aside.

Wash the radish and trim off the outer leaves. Transfer to a cutting board and chop into small pieces. Place in a large salad bowl and set aside.

Wash the cucumber and cut into thin slices.

Combine cucumber with the radish and drizzle all with the previously prepared dressing. Toss to combine and serve immediately.

Enjoy!

Nutritional information per serving: Kcal: 67, Protein: 2.9g, Carbs: 13.4g, Fats: 1.1g

28. Steamed Spinach Salad

Ingredients:

4 oz fresh spinach, chopped

1 tsp apple cider vinegar

1 tbsp extra-virgin olive oil

¼ tsp salt

¼ tsp Italian seasoning

¼ tsp black pepper, ground

Preparation:

Using a large colander, rinse the spinach under cold running water. Drain and chop into small pieces.

In a small mixing bowl, combine apple cider vinegar, olive oil, salt, Italian seasoning, and pepper. Mix until combined and set aside.

Pour 1 cup of water in a deep pot. Bring to a boil over medium-high heat. Place the spinach in a steam basket. Place the basket on top of the pot and cook for 5 minutes, or until wilted. Remove from the heat and transfer to a serving dish.

Drizzle with previously prepared dressing and serve immediately.

Enjoy!

Nutritional information per serving: Kcal: 152, Protein: 3.3g, Carbs: 4.6g, Fats: 14.8g

29. Red Cabbage Tomato Salad

Ingredients:

2 cups fresh cabbage, thinly shredded

½ cup plum tomatoes, chopped

¼ cup apple cider vinegar

¼ tsp dried thyme, ground

¼ tsp dried oregano, ground

2 tbsp olive oil

Salt and pepper

Preparation:

In a small mixing bowl, combine apple cider vinegar, dried thyme, dried oregano, olive oil, salt, and pepper. Mix until combined and set aside.

Rinse the cabbage under running water. Transfer to a cutting board and shred into thin strips. Transfer to a large bowl and set aside.

Rinse the tomatoes and remove the stems. Chop into bite-sized pieces and add to the bowl with cabbage.

Drizzle all with previously prepared dressing and serve

immediately

Enjoy!

Nutritional information per serving: Kcal: 155, Protein: 1.5g, Carbs: 6.9g, Fats: 14.2g

30. Turkey Pepper Salad

Ingredients:

4 oz turkey breast, skinless and boneless

1 large red bell pepper, chopped

1 large yellow bell pepper, chopped

1 cucumber, chunked

1 small purple onion, diced

1 tbsp olive oil

1 tbsp white wine vinegar

½ tsp dried thyme, ground

¼ tsp dried rosemary, ground

2 tbsp lime juice, freshly squeezed

Salt and pepper

Preparation:

Rinse the meat under running water and pat-dry with a kitchen towel. Transfer to a cutting board and cut into thin slices.

Place the meat in a deep pot and add water enough to

cover. Bring to a boil over medium-high heat. Cook for 10-15 minutes, or until fork-tender. Remove from the heat and set aside. Optionally, place on a grill for 2 minutes on each side to get nicely golden brown color.

In a small mixing bowl, combine olive oil, white wine vinegar, dried thyme, dried rosemary, lime juice, salt, and pepper. Mix until well combined and set aside.

Wash and prepare the remaining ingredients.

In a large salad bowl, combine bell pepper, cucumber, and onion. Top with turkey slices and drizzle all with previously prepared dressing.

Serve immediately.

Nutritional information per serving: Kcal: 206, Protein: 12.5g, Carbs: 24.1g, Fats: 8.5g

31. Spinach Egg Salad

Ingredients:

2 cups fresh spinach, chopped

1 large egg, hard-boiled

1 small onion, sliced

¼ cup ricotta cheese, crumbled

1 small cucumber, sliced

1 tsp balsamic vinegar

1 tbsp olive oil

2 garlic cloves, crushed

¼ tsp smoked paprika

Salt and pepper

Preparation:

Place the egg in a deep pot and add enough water to cover. Bring to a boil over medium-high heat. Cook for 10-12 minutes. Remove from the heat and transfer to the prepared ice cold water bath. Let it sit for 5 minutes to chill.

Meanwhile, rinse the spinach under running water and

drain. Chop into small pieces and set aside.

Pour 1 cup of water in a deep pot. Bring to a boil over medium-high heat. Place the spinach in a steam basket. Place the basket on top of the pot and steam for 3-5 minutes, or until wilted. Remove from the heat and transfer to a large salad bowl.

In a small mixing bowl, combine balsamic vinegar, olive oil, garlic, smoked paprika, salt, and pepper. Mix until well combined.

Peel the egg and cut into thin wedges. Add to the bowl with spinach, along with onion and cucumber. Drizzle all with previously prepared dressing and top with ricotta cheese.

Serve cold.

Nutritional information per serving: Kcal: 188, Protein: 9.1g, Carbs: 12.8g, Fats: 12.3g

32. Roasted Beet Salad with Walnuts

Ingredients:

1 large beet, sliced

2 cups fresh arugula, chopped

¼ cup goat's cheese, crumbled

½ ripe avocado, sliced

1 tbsp olive oil

1 tbsp red wine vinegar

2 tbsp walnuts, roughly chopped

Salt and pepper

Preparation:

Preheat the grill to medium-high heat.

Wash the beets and trim off the green parts. Cut into thin slices and brush with some olive oil. Sprinkle with some salt and pepper.

Grill the beets for 4-5 minutes on each side. Remove to a plate and set aside.

Rinse the arugula under running water. Drain and torn into

small pieces. Place in a large salad bowl and set aside.

In a small mixing bowl, combine olive oil, red wine vinegar, salt, and pepper. Mix until combined and set aside.

Now, combine arugula, beets, avocado, and goat's cheese in a bowl. Mix until combined and then drizzle with previously prepared dressing. Toss to combine and top with walnuts before serving.

Enjoy!

Nutritional information per serving: Kcal: 228, Protein: 6.9g, Carbs: 7.8g, Fats: 20.1g

33. Avocado Salad with Pickled Onions

Ingredients:

1 ripe avocado, sliced

¼ cup black beans, cooked

1 medium-sized purple onion, sliced

2 tbsp fresh parsley, finely chopped

2 tbsp balsamic vinegar

1 tsp coconut syrup

½ cup cherry tomatoes

¼ tsp cumin powder

1 whole lime, juiced

1 tbsp olive oil

Salt and pepper

Preparation:

Peel the onion and cut into thin slices. Place in a small bowl and drizzle with balsamic vinegar, coconut syrup, and some salt. Let it marinate for 15 minutes. Stir occasionally.

Cut the avocado lengthwise in half. Peel and remove the

pit. Cut into bite-sized pieces and set aside.

In a large salad bowl, combine avocado, beans, parsley, and pickled onions. Add the remaining marinade from the onions. Sprinkle all with cumin powder and lime juice. Add a pinch of salt and pepper and give it a good stir.

Serve immediately.

Nutritional information per serving: Kcal: 265, Protein: 5.6g, Carbs: 23.3g, Fats: 18.1g

34. Quinoa Salad with Spicy Vinaigrette

Ingredients:

½ cup quinoa

1 small cucumber, sliced

1 cup cherry tomatoes, chopped

¼ cup Feta cheese, crumbled

2 tbsp olive oil

1 tbsp red wine vinegar

1 garlic clove, minced

½ tsp red pepper flakes

¼ tsp smoked paprika

¼ tsp dried oregano, ground

Salt and pepper

Preparation:

Place the quinoa in a medium saucepan and add 1 cup of water. Bring to a boil over medium-high heat. Cook for 12-15 minutes, or until all the liquid has been soaked up and evaporated. Remove from the heat and fluff with a wooden spoon. Set aside.

In a small mixing bowl, combine olive oil, red wine vinegar, garlic, red pepper flakes, smoked paprika, dried oregano, salt, and pepper. Mix until well combined and set aside.

Wash and prepare the remaining ingredients.

In a large salad bowl, combine cooked quinoa, cucumber, cherry tomatoes, and feta cheese. Drizzle all with previously prepared dressing and give it a good stir.

Optionally, drizzle with some fresh lemo juice.

Enjoy!

Nutritional information per serving: Kcal: 186, Protein: 5.3g, Carbs: 19g, Fats: 10.5g

35. Greek Salad with Kalamata Olives

Ingredients:

1 cup grape tomatoes, halved

1 large cucumber, sliced

1 small purple onion, sliced

¼ cup Feta cheese, crumbled

¼ cup Kalamata olives, pitted and sliced

1 tbsp balsamic vinegar

2 tbsp olive oil

1 whole lemon, juiced

½ tsp dried oregano, ground

¼ tsp dried rosemary, ground

1 tbsp fresh parsley, finely chopped

½ tsp black pepper, freshly ground

½ tsp kosher salt

Preparation:

Rinse the tomatoes under running water. Cut each in half

and place in a large salad bowl. Set aside.

Wash the cucumber and lengthwise in half. Cut into thin slices and add to the bowl.

Peel the onion and cut into small pieces. Add to the bowl with the remaining ingredients.

In a small mixing bowl, combine balsamic vinegar, olive oil, lemon juice, dried oregano, dried rosemary, parsley, black pepper, and salt. Mix until combined and set aside.

Now, add cheese and olives to the remaining ingredients and drizzle all with previously prepared dressing. Toss to combine and serve immediately.

Enjoy!

Nutritional information per serving: Kcal: 247, Protein: 5.1g, Carbs: 14.9g, Fats: 20.3g

36. Balsamic Steak Salad with Peaches

Ingredients:

4 oz lean skirt steak, thinly sliced

1 large peach, wedged

2 cups fresh arugula, chopped

¼ cup blue cheese, crumbled

¼ cup balsamic vinegar

1 garlic clove, crushed

1 tbsp olive oil

1 whole lime, freshly squeezed

Salt and pepper

Preparation:

Rinse well the meat and pat-dry with a kitchen towel. Transfer to a cutting board and cut into thin slices. Place in a deep bowl and add balsamic vinegar, garlic, salt, and pepper. Let it marinate for 20 minutes.

Meanwhile, preheat the grill to medium-high heat. Grill the steak for 3-5 minutes on each side.

Rinse the arugula thoroughly under running water. Drain and chop into small pieces. Set aside.

In a small mixing bowl, combine olive oil, lime juice, salt, and pepper. Mix until combined and set aside.

In a large mixing bowl, combine arugula, blue cheese, and peach. Top with steaks and sprinkle with previously prepared dressing.

Toss to combine and serve immediately.

Nutritional information per serving: Kcal: 193, Protein: 13.5g, Carbs: 8.3g, Fats: 12g

37. Chickpea Salad with Wild Garlic

Ingredients:

1 cup canned chickpeas, drained and rinsed

1 small red bell pepper, chopped

1 small cucumber, chopped

½ cup spring onions, chopped

¼ cup wild garlic, finely chopped

¼ cup cottage cheese, crumbled

2 tbsp olive oil

1 tbsp apple cider vinegar

2 tbsp lemon juice, freshly squeezed

1 tbsp fresh parsley, finely chopped

¼ tsp red pepper flakes

Salt and pepper

Preparation:

Place the chickpeas in a colander and rinse well. Drain and set aside.

Cut the bell pepper lengthwise in half. Remove the stem and seeds. Chop into small pieces and set aside.

Wash the cucumber and cut into thin slices. Set aside.

Rinse the wild garlic leaves under running water. Torn into small pieces and set aside.

In a small mixing bowl, combine olive oil, apple cider vinegar, lemon juice, parsley, salt, and pepper. Mix until combined and set aside.

In a large salad bowl, combine chickpeas, red bell pepper, cucumber, spring onions, wild garlic, and cottage cheese. Drizzle with previously prepared dressing and toss to combine.

Serve immediately.

Nutritional information per serving: Kcal: 230, Protein: 8.1g, Carbs: 27.1g, Fats: 11g

38. Spinach Pecorino Salad

Ingredients:

2 cups baby spinach, chopped

¼ cup Pecorino cheese, grated

1 medium-sized Granny Smith's apple, cored and chopped

2 tbsp lemon juice, freshly squeezed

1 tbsp balsamic vinegar

1 tsp lime zest, freshly grated

Salt and pepper

Preparation:

Place the spinach in a large colander and rinse under running water. Drain and chop into small pieces. Set aside.

Wash the apple and cut in half. Remove the core and cut into thin slices. Set aside.

In a small mixing bowl, combine lemon juice, balsamic vinegar, lime zest, salt, and pepper. Mix until combined and set aside.

In a large salad bowl, combine baby spinach, Pecorino cheese, and apple. Drizzle with previously prepared dressing and toss to combine.

Optionally, sprinkle with some pomegranate seeds before serving.

Enjoy!

Nutritional information per serving: Kcal: 205, Protein: 10g, Carbs: 25.3g, Fats: 8.5g

39. Chicken Salad with Pecans

Ingredients:

4 oz chicken breast, skinless and boneless

½ cup grapes

¼ cup spring onions, chopped

1 cup Romaine lettuce, chopped

2 tbsp pecans, roughly chopped

¼ cup Greek yogurt

2 tbsp lemon juice, freshly squeezed

1 tsp Dijon mustard

1 tbsp fresh dill, finely chopped

1 tbsp fresh parsley, finely chopped

¼ tsp smoked paprika

Salt and pepper

Preparation:

Preheat the grill to medium-high heat.

In a mixing bowl, combine Greek yogurt, lemon juice, Dijon

mustard, dill, parsley, smoked paprika, salt, and pepper. Mix until combined and set aside.

Rinse the chicken and pat-dry with a kitchen towel. Sprinkle with some salt and pepper and grill for 3 minutes on each side.

Now, place chicken in a deep bowl along with grapes and pecans. Drizzle with yogurt mixture and mix until all well coated

Serve immediately.

Nutritional information per serving: Kcal: 201, Protein: 11.4g, Carbs: 7.8g, Fats: 14.7g

40. Green Bean Fusilli Salad

Ingredients:

4 oz. fusilli pasta

1 cup green beans

¼ cup Feta cheese, crumbled

¼ cup olives, pitted and chopped

2 garlic cloves, minced

½ onion, finely chopped

1 cup yogurt, low-fat

1 tsp. yellow mustard

2 tbsp. olive oil

½ tsp. dried dill, ground

½ tsp. red pepper, ground

Salt

Preparation:

Place the pasta in a deep pot. Add enough water to cover and bring it to a boil. Sprinkle with some salt and cook for 10 minutes over medium-high heat. Remove from the heat and transfer to a large colander. Rinse under cold running water and set aside. Place the green beans in a deep pot and cover with water. Bring to a boil over medium-high heat and cook for 5 minutes. Remove from the heat and drain. Set aside. Preheat one tablespoon of olive oil in a large skillet over medium-high heat. Add onions and garlic. Stir-fry for 2-3 minutes, or until translucent. Add green beans and cook for 5 minutes. Remove from the heat and transfer to a large salad bowl. Add pasta to the bowl and stir well. Set aside.

Now, combine the remaining olive oil, yogurt, mustard, dried dill, red pepper, and a pinch of salt in a mixing bowl. Mix until well combined and pour over prepared beans and pasta. Top with olives and cheese before serving.

Nutritional information per serving: Kcal: 264, Protein: 9.3g, Carbs: 31.5g, Fats: 11.2g

41. Cooked Celery Salad

Ingredients:

4 celery sticks, with leaves

1 whole lemon, juiced

3 tbsp. walnuts, halved

1 small purple onion, finely chopped

2 tbsp. white wine vinegar

2 cups lamb's lettuce, roughly chopped

1 tsp. flaxseed oil

½ tsp. salt

½ tsp. black pepper, ground

Preparation:

Rinse the celery under cold running water and drain. Transfer to a cutting board and separate sticks and leaves. Chop the sticks into strips and finely chop the leaves. Set aside.

Transfer the celery sticks in a deep pot. Cover with water and bring to a boil over medium-high heat. Cook for 8 minutes. Add celery leaves and fresh lemon juice. Stir once and cook for 2-3 minutes more. Remove from the heat and drain. Rinse all under cold running water immediately. Set aside.

In a mixing bowl, combine onions, vinegar, salt, and pepper. Mix until well incorporated. Add flaxseed oil and mix again until combined.

Now, arrange the lamb's lettuce over a serving dish and top with celery. Drizzle with previously prepared dressing.

Serve cold.

Nutritional information per serving: Kcal: 273, Protein: 8.8g, Carbs: 17.9g, Fats: 19g

42. Avocado Egg Salad

Ingredients:

1 ripe avocado, cut into cubes

2 large eggs, hard-boiled

2 spring onions, chopped

½ cup Greek yogurt

1 tbsp. sour cream

1 whole lime, juiced

1 tsp. fresh thyme, finely chopped

Salt and pepper to taste

Preparation:

Place the eggs in a deep pot. Add water enough to cover and bring to a boil over medium-high heat. Cook for 10-12 minutes. Remove from the heat and transfer to a bowl with ice cold water. You can add a few ice cubes to speed up the process. Peel and cut into bite-sized pieces. Set aside.

Peel the avocado and cut lengthwise in half. Remove the pit and cut into bite-sized cubes. Set aside.

In a mixing bowl, combine Greek yogurt, sour cream, lime

juice, thyme, salt, and pepper. Mix until combined.

In a serving bowl, combine eggs and avocado. Drizzle with previously prepared dressing and give it a good stir.

Serve immediately.

Nutritional information per serving: Kcal: 343, Protein: 14g, Carbs: 16.3g, Fats: 27g

43. Grilled Mustard Turkey Salad

Ingredients:

8 oz. turkey breast, skinless and boneless

1 tbsp. yellow mustard

3 tsp. olive oil

½ tsp. salt

½ tsp. black pepper, ground

2 cups Romaine lettuce, chopped

1 cup lamb's lettuce

½ cup cherry tomatoes, chopped

1 tbsp. Parmesan cheese, shredded

2 tsp. red wine vinegar

Preparation:

Rinse and drain the turkey breast. Transfer to a cutting board and cut into thin slices. Set aside.

In a small mixing bowl, combine 2 teaspoons of olive oil, salt, black pepper, and mustard. Mix until combined and pour over the meat. Rub with your hands to allow flavors to penetrate into the meat. Cover the dish with a plastic foil and refrigerate for 1 hour.

Preheat the grill to medium-high. Add meat and grill for 3-4 minutes on each side. Remove from the heat and transfer to a cutting board. Let it chill for a while and then cut into strips.

Wash and prepare the vegetables.

In a large salad bowl, combine lettuce, lamb's lettuce, and cherry tomatoes. Top with turkey strips and drizzle with red wine vinegar. Sprinkle with parmesan cheese and serve immediately.

Nutritional information per serving: Kcal: 248, Protein: 25g, Carbs: 9.6g, Fats: 12.4g

44. Shrimp Avocado Salad

Ingredients:

4 oz. shrimps, cleaned and deveined

½ ripe avocado, chopped

¼ cup Feta cheese, crumbled

1 medium-sized green bell pepper, chopped

½ cup cherry tomatoes, chopped

½ cup fresh mint, roughly chopped

1 small purple onion, chopped

¼ cup green olives, pitted

1 tbsp. fresh parsley, finely chopped

1 whole lime, juiced

¼ tsp. garlic powder

¼ tsp. dried oregano, ground

½ tsp. red pepper flakes

2 tbsp. olive oil

Salt to taste

Preparation:

In a small mixing bowl, combine lime juice, oregano, garlic, 1 tablespoon of olive oil, pepper flakes, and salt. Mix until well combined and set aside.

Wash and prepare the vegetables.

In a large salad bowl, combine cherry tomatoes, mint, purple onion, green olives, and parsley. Drizzle with previously prepared dressing and refrigerate for 20 minutes.

Preheat the remaining oil in a skillet over medium-high heat. Add shrimps and sprinkle with some salt and red pepper. Cook for 2-3 minutes, or until set. Remove from the heat and set aside to chill for a while.

Now, add cheese and avocado to the salad. Mix again and top with shrimps. Garnish with fresh mint and serve immediately.

Nutritional information per serving: Kcal: 264, Protein: 12.6g, Carbs: 12.2g, Fats: 19.6g

45. Chicken Celery Salad

Ingredients:

6 oz. chicken thighs, skinless and boneless

2 tbsp. dried cranberries

2 medium-sized celery sticks, chopped

4 spring onions, chopped

2 tbsp. Greek yogurt

1 tbsp. sour cream

1 tbsp. olive oil

½ tsp. dried oregano, ground

¼ tsp. dried thyme, ground

Salt and pepper to taste

Preparation:

Rinse the chicken under cold running water and pat-dry with a kitchen paper. Transfer to a cutting board and chop into bite-sized pieces.

Rinse the celery and discard the leaves. Cut the sticks into small pieces and set aside.

Rinse the spring onions and chop into small pieces. Set aside.

Preheat the oil in medium skillet over medium-high heat. Add chicken and sprinkle with some salt and pepper. Cook for 3-5 minutes, or until golden brown. Remove from the heat and set aside.

Now, combine chicken, celery, and spring onions in a large salad bowl.

In a small mixing bowl, combine Greek yogurt, sour cream, dried oregano, dried thyme, salt, and pepper. Mix until well combined and drizzle over the salad. Give it a good stir and serve immediately.

Optionally, garnish with lime or lemon slices.

Nutritional information per serving: Kcal: 275, Protein: 28.2g, Carbs: 5.6g, Fats: 15.2g

46. Butternut Squash Salad with Feta and Arugula

Ingredients:

2 cups butternut squash, cubed

¼ cup Feta cheese, crumbled

2 cups arugula, roughly chopped

1 tbsp. extra-virgin olive oil

½ tsp. salt

½ tsp. black pepper, ground

½ tsp. Italian seasoning

Preparation:

Preheat the oven to 350 degrees. Line some parchment paper over a baking sheet and set aside.

Cut the squash lengthwise in half. Using a tablespoon, scoop out the seeds and inner soft flesh. Peel and cut into bite-sized cubes. Fill the measuring cups and reserve the rest in the refrigerator.

Spread the squash over a prepared baking sheet. Sprinkle with some olive oil, salt, and Italian seasoning. Bake for about 30-40 minutes. Remove to a wire rack and let it chill completely.

Rinse the arugula under cold running water. Drain and roughly chop into small pieces.

Now, combine squash, arugula, and cheese in a salad bowl. Optionally, drizzle with some lemon juice and serve immediately.

Enjoy!

Nutritional information per serving: Kcal: 182, Protein: 4.6g, Carbs: 18.3g, Fats: 11.6g

47. Spinach Potato Salad with Apple

Ingredients:

2 cups baby spinach, torn

2 Granny Smith's apple, chopped

1 tbsp. walnuts, finely chopped

1 cup fresh arugula, torn

¼ cup goat's cheese, crumbled

½ whole lemon, juiced

1 tbsp. apple cider vinegar

Salt and pepper to taste

Preparation:

Combine spinach and arugula in a large colander. Rinse under cold running water and drain. Torn into small pieces and set aside.

Wash the apples and cut lengthwise in half. Remove the core and cut into bite-sized pieces.

Now, combine spinach, arugula, and apples in a large salad bowl. Add goat's cheese and top with walnuts.

Sprinkle all with lemon juice, apple cider vinegar, salt, and pepper. Give it a good stir and serve immediately.

Nutritional information per serving: Kcal: 241, Protein: 8.7g, Carbs: 33.7g, Fats: 9.9g

48. Garlic Pasta Salad

Ingredients:

1 medium-sized garlic head

4 oz. pasta of your choice

1 cup ricotta cheese

1 tbsp. Parmesan cheese

½ cup cherry tomatoes, chopped

1 cup fresh spinach, torn

1 tbsp. olive oil

Salt and pepper to taste

Preparation:

Place the garlic in a microwave-safe bowl. Sprinkle with olive oil, salt, and pepper. Microwave for 2 minutes, or until tender. Remove from the microwave and set aside to chill for a while.

Place the pasta in a deep pot and add water enough to cover. Bring to a boil over medium-high heat. Cook for 10 minutes and remove from the heat. Drain well and set aside.

Now, make the dressing. Peel the garlic and place in a small mixing bowl along with salt and pepper. Crush with a fork and then add ricotta cheese. Mix until all well combined. Optionally, add some warm water if the mixture is too thick.

Now, transfer pasta to a serving bowl. Add cherry tomatoes, spinach, and parmesan cheese. Give it a good stir and then drizzle with previously prepared dressing.

Stir again and serve immediately.

Nutritional information per serving: Kcal: 313, Protein: 17.8g, Carbs: 29.4g, Fats: 14.2g

49. Kale Salad with Blueberry Sauce

Ingredients:

2 cups fresh kale, chopped

1 cup blueberries

½ cup Mozzarella cheese, sliced

1 cup cherry tomatoes, chopped

½ tsp. salt

1 tbsp. balsamic vinegar

1 tsp. honey

1 tsp. yellow mustard

3 tbsp. olive oil

Salt and pepper to taste

Preparation:

In a food processor, combine ½ cup of blueberries, balsamic vinegar, honey, yellow mustard, olive oil, salt, and pepper. Pulse until smooth and creamy. Set aside.

Using a large colander, rinse the kale under cold running water. Drain and transfer to a cutting board. Discard all hard stems and chop into small pieces.

Now, combine cherry tomatoes, cheese, and kale in a large salad bowl. Drizzle all with previously prepared dressing.

Finally, top all with the remaining blueberries and serve immediately.

Enjoy!

Nutritional information per serving: Kcal: 305, Protein: 5.5g, Carbs: 24.3g, Fats: 22.8g

50. Spicy Watermelon Kohlrabi Salad

Ingredients:

2 cups watermelon, cubed

1 medium-sized kohlrabi, cubed

1 small chili pepper, chopped

3 spring onions, chopped

¼ cup Feta cheese, crumbled

1 whole lime, juiced

2 tbsp. fresh coriander, finely chopped

1 tbsp. fresh mint, finely chopped

Salt and pepper

Preparation:

Cut the watermelon lengthwise in half. Cut one large wedge and chop into bite-sized pieces. Remove the seeds and set aside. Wrap the remaining watermelon in a plastic foil and refrigerate for later.

Rinse the kohlrabi under running water and drain. Remove the outer damaged leaves and cut into small cubes. Set aside.

Rinse the spring onions and remove the green parts. Use only white and light green stem. Chop into small pieces and set aside.

In a serving salad bowl, combine watermelon, kohlrabi, spring onions, chili pepper, Feta cheese, coriander, and mint. Drizzle all with lime juice. Add some salt to taste and give it a good stir.

Serve immediately.

Nutritional information per serving: Kcal: 266, Protein: 11g, Carbs: 44g, Fats: 8.8g

51. Barley Bean Salad

Ingredients:

1 cup barley

1 cup black beans, soaked overnight

1 small purple onion, chopped

1 large red bell pepper, chopped

2 medium-sized tomatoes

½ tsp. dried basil, ground

½ tsp. dried oregano, ground

½ tsp. dried dill, ground

Salt and pepper to taste

Preparation:

Drain the beans and place in a deep pot. Add 2 cups of water and bring to a boil over medium-high heat. Cook for 20-30 minutes, or until tender. Remove from the heat and drain. Set aside.

Place the barley in a deep pot of boiling water. Sprinkle with some salt and cook for 20 minutes. Remove from the heat and let it chill for a while.

Wash and prepare the vegetables.

In a salad bowl, combine red bell pepper, onion, tomatoes, beans, and barley. Sprinkle all with basil, oregano, dill, salt and pepper. Mix until well combined and serve.

Enjoy!

Nutritional information per serving: Kcal: 357, Protein: 17.3g, Carbs: 70.5g, Fats: 2g

52. Baked Pepper Salad with Garlic Dressing

Ingredients:

5 large bell peppers

2 garlic cloves, finely chopped

1 tbsp. fresh parsley, finely chopped

2 tbsp. olive oil

1 tbsp. apple cider vinegar

½ tsp. fresh thyme, finely chopped

Salt and pepper to taste

Preparation:

Preheat the oven to 350 degrees. Line some parchment paper over a baking sheet and set aside.

Wash the bell peppers and pat-dry with a kitchen paper. Poke with a fork few time and spread over the prepared baking sheet.

Bake for 10-12 minutes on each side, or until nicely golden brown. When done, remove from the oven and set aside to cool completely. Now, peel the skin and transfer to a serving dish.

In a small mixing bowl, combine olive oil, apple cider vinegar, garlic, thyme, salt, and pepper. Mix until well combined. Drizzle over the peppers and stir well.

Finally, sprinkle with parsley and serve immediately.

Nutritional information per serving: Kcal: 222, Protein: 3.3g, Carbs: 23.8g, Fats: 14.8g

MEAL RECIPES

1. Salmon with Brown Rice

Ingredients:

1 lbs of salmon fillets, thinly sliced

1 cup of brown rice, pre-cooked

1 tbsp of olive oil

1 tsp of fresh rosemary, finely chopped

3 cups of water

1 tsp of sea salt

¼ tsp of black pepper, ground

Preparation:

Wash and pat dry the salmon fillets. Dry with a kitchen paper and set aside.

Place the rice in a deep pot. Add 3 cups of water and bring it to a boil. Cook for about 12-15 minutes and then remove from the heat. Sprinkle with some salt and stir well. Set aside.

Preheat the oil in a large saucepan over a medium-high temperature. Add fillets and sprinkle with some salt, pepper, and rosemary. Cook for about 3-4 minutes on each side. Remove from the heat.

Serve fillets with rice. You can add some more steamed vegetables, but this is optional.

Enjoy!

Nutrition information per serving: Kcal: 283, Protein: 20.5g, Carbs: 29.2g, Fats: 9.5g

2. Peanut Orange Quinoa

Ingredients:

1 cup of quinoa

¼ cup of dried figs, chopped

1 large orange, peeled and wedged

¼ tsp of cinnamon, ground

1 tbsp of peanuts, roughly chopped

1 cup of water

Preparation:

Combine quinoa and water in a pot and bring it to a boil. Reduce the heat to low and cook for about 12-15 minutes. Remove from the heat and fluff the quinoa with a fork. Set aside.

Peel the orange and divide into wedges. Cut 2-3 wedges into small pieces. Transfer the rest of the orange in a juicer. Process until juiced and set aside.

Now, combine cooked quinoa, figs, and orange wedges. Drizzle with fresh orange juice and sprinkle with peanuts. Stir all well and set aside for 5 minutes to allow flavors to meld.

Enjoy!

Nutrition information per serving: Kcal: 445, Protein: 14.9g, Carbs: 82.2g, Fats: 7.7g

3.   Cherry Tomato Spring Salad

Ingredients:

5 cherry tomatoes, halved

2 cups of Romaine lettuce, shredded

½ cup of fresh kale, roughly chopped

1 large red bell pepper, chopped

2 garlic cloves, minced

1 small onion, sliced

4 tbsp of olive oil

1 tbsp of apple cider vinegar

1 tsp of Himalayan pink salt

¼ tsp of Cayenne pepper, ground

¼ tsp of black pepper, freshly ground

Preparation:

In a small bowl, combine olive oil, vinegar, garlic, salt, cayenne, and pepper. Mix well until incorporated. Set aside for 15 minutes to allow flavors to blend.

Wash the cherry tomatoes and cut in half. Place them in a

large bowl and set aside.

Using a colander, wash the lettuce and kale under cold running water. Shred the lettuce and kale and add it to the bowl with tomatoes.

Wash the bell pepper and cut in half. Remove the seeds and cut into small pieces or rings.

Peel the onion and cut into thin slices. Add to the bowl with other ingredients.

Drizzle with previously prepared dressing and toss well to coat.

Serve immediately.

Nutrition information per serving: Kcal: 234, Protein: 3.1g, Carbs: 16.3g, Fats: 19.3g

4. Brussels Sprouts Rice Casserole

Ingredients:

10 oz of Brussels sprouts, chopped

1 cup of brown rice, pre-cooked

2 cups of chicken stock

3 oz of Mozzarella cheese, crumbled

¼ tsp of Cayenne pepper, ground

1 small red onion, chopped

1 tbsp of vegetable oil

1 tsp of salt

¼ tsp of black pepper, ground

Preparation:

Preheat the oven to 375°F.

Place the rice in a heavy-bottomed pot. Add 3 cups of water and bring it to a boil. Reduce the heat to low and cook for about 12-15 minutes. Remove from the heat and fluff with a fork. Cover with a lid and set aside.

In a large bowl, combine chicken stock, cheese, and onion.

Season with salt, pepper and cayenne and stir well. Set aside.

Wash the Brussels sprouts and trim off the outer leaves. Cut into bite-sized pieces and transfer to a baking sheet. Steam for about 5-7 minutes and then transfer to greased casserole dish. Add rice and slightly stir to allow rice to coat the Brussels sprouts. Pour over the stock mixture and place it in the oven.

Bake for about 30-35 minutes and then remove from the heat. Allow it to cool for a while before serving.

Nutrition information per serving: Kcal: 239, Protein: 9.3g, Carbs: 36.3g, Fats: 6.9g

5. Pineapple Raspberry Salad

Ingredients:

1 cup of pineapple chunks

1 cup of fresh raspberries

1 cup of watermelon, cubed

1 large green apple, cored and chopped

4 tbsp of coconut water

2 tbsp of sour cream

1 tsp of vanilla extract

4 tbsp of orange juice

1 tbsp of fresh mint

Preparation:

In a medium mixing bowl, combine sour cream, coconut water, vanilla extract, and orange juice. Stir well to blend and set aside to allow flavors to meld.

Wash and prepare the fruits.

In a large salad bowl, combine pineapple chunks, raspberries, watermelon, and apple. Mix once and then drizzle with previously prepared dressing. Give it a good final stir and refrigerate for 20 minutes before serving.

Enjoy!

Nutritional information per serving: Kcal: 207, Protein: 2.8g, Carbs: 44.6g, Fats: 3.5g

6. Celery Spinach Soup

Ingredients:

1 lb of fresh celery, chopped

1 lb of fresh spinach, chopped

1 medium-sized red onion, finely chopped

1 cup of heavy cream

1 cup of water

1 cup of sour cream

2 cups of vegetable broth

2 tbsp of butter

½ tsp of dried thyme, ground

½ tsp of salt

½ tsp of black pepper, ground

Preparation:

Combine celery and spinach in a large colander. Wash thoroughly under cold running water. Drain and chop into small pieces. Set aside.

Melt the butter in a large saucepan over a medium-high

temperature. Add onions and stir-fry until translucent. Add celery and spinach. Sprinkle with salt, thyme and pepper. Stir well and cook for about 3-4 minutes, or until celery and spinach tender.

Add the vegetable broth and water. Stir well and bring it to a boil. Reduce the heat to low and cover with a lid. Cook for 15-20 minutes and then stir in the heavy cream and sour cream. Cook for another 5 minutes and remove from the heat.

Cover with a lid and cook for 20 minutes. Remove from the heat and stir in the heavy cream.

Serve immediately.

Nutrition information per serving: Kcal: 235, Protein: 6.2g, Carbs: 9.4g, Fats: 20.2g

7. Peanut Lemon Risotto

Ingredients:

2 cups of basmati rice

1 small red onion, chopped

1 garlic clove, finely chopped

½ cup of fresh kale, chopped

1 tbsp of olive oil

1 large lime, freshly squeezed

3 tbsp of peanuts, roughly chopped

3 ½ cups of water

¼ tsp of black pepper, ground

¼ tsp of chili pepper, ground

½ tsp of sea salt

Preparation:

Place the rice in a heavy-bottomed pot. Add water and bring it to a boil. Cook for about 12-15 minutes and remove from the heat. Cover with a lid and set aside.

Preheat the oil in a large skillet over a medium-high

temperature. Add onions and garlic. Stir-fry for about 4-5 minutes, or until translucent. Add kale and cook for 5 more minutes. Add about ½ cup of water and bring it to a boil. Sprinkle with salt and pepper.

Stir in the rice and cook for 2 more minutes. Remove from the heat and stir in the peanuts and chili pepper.

Serve warm.

Nutrition information per serving: Kcal: 424, Protein: 9g, Carbs: 79.7g, Fats: 7.5g

8. Cod with Sweet Potatoes and Spinach

Ingredients:

1 lb of cod fillets, cut into bite-sized pieces

2 tbsp of olive oil

1 tbsp of basil, finely chopped

1 cup of spinach, chopped

1 cup of sweet potatoes

1 small onion, chopped

1 tbsp of balsamic vinegar

1 tsp of sea salt

¼ tsp of black pepper, ground

Preparation:

Peel the sweet potato and cut into bite-sized cubes. Place in a deep pot of boiling water and cook until fork-tender. Remove from the heat and drain well. Set aside.

Preheat 1 tablespoon of oil in a frying pan and add onions. Stir-fry until translucent and then add potatoes. Sprinkle with vinegar, basil, salt, and pepper. Stir well and cook for 2 minutes until well incorporated. Remove from the heat and set aside.

Preheat the remaining oil in a large skillet over a medium-high temperature. Add fillets and sprinkle with some salt and pepper. Cook for about 3-5 minutes, or until golden brown. Remove from the heat.

Serve the cod chops with previously prepared vegetables.

Enjoy!

Nutrition information per serving: Kcal: 233, Protein: 26.9g, Carbs: 12.5g, Fats: 8.1g

9. Cherry Banana Oatmeal

Ingredients:

½ cup of fresh cherries, pitted

1 medium-sized banana, sliced

1 cup of rolled oats

1 cup of skim milk

1 tbsp of almonds, roughly chopped

Preparation:

Using a colander, wash the cherries under cold running water. Drain and cut in half. Remove the pits and set aside.

Peel the banana and cut into thin slices. Set aside.

Pour the water in a heavy-bottomed pot. Bring it to a boil and then add oats. Cook for about 3-4 minutes, stirring constantly. Remove from the heat and let it soak for 10 minutes. Fluff with a fork to allow it to cool faster.

Stir in the cherries, banana, and milk. Top with almonds and serve.

Enjoy!

Nutrition information per serving: Kcal: 316, Protein: 10.8g, Carbs: 6.3g, Fats: 4.4g

10. Chicken in Tomato-Garlic Sauce

Ingredients:

1 lb of chicken fillets, thinly sliced

1 large tomato, cut into bite-sized pieces

1 cup of fresh arugula, chopped

1 tbsp of olive oil

2 garlic cloves, finely chopped

1 large lemon, freshly squeezed

1 tbsp of balsamic vinegar

½ tsp of salt

¼ tsp of black pepper, ground

¼ tsp of cayenne pepper, ground

Preparation:

Wash the chicken fillets under cold running water and pat dry with a kitchen paper. Set aside.

Preheat the oil in a large skillet over a medium-high temperature. Add fillets and reduce the heat to medium. Sprinkle with salt, pepper, and cayenne. Cook for about 3-

4 minutes on each side.

Meanwhile, combine lime juice, vinegar and ¼ cup of water. Mix and pour over the fillets. Bring it to a boil, then add garlic and tomatoes.

Saute for 5 minutes, or until tomatoes soften. Remove from the heat and set aside.

Make a sheet of arugula on a serving plate and top with fillets. Spoon the remaining liquid over the fillets and serve.

Enjoy!

Nutrition information per serving: Kcal: 350, Protein: 44.8g, Carbs: 5.3g, Fats: 16.1g

11. Spinach Blackberry Smoothie

Ingredients:

1 cup of fresh spinach, chopped

1 cup of blackberries

½ cup of Greek yogurt

2 tbsp of lemon juice, freshly squeezed

1 tbsp of honey

1 tbsp of chia seeds

Preparation:

Wash the spinach thoroughly under cold running water. Roughly chop it and set aside.

Using a colander, rinse the blackberries and slightly drain. Set aside.

Now, combine spinach, blackberries, yogurt, and lemon juice in a blender or a food processor. Process until nicely smooth and creamy. Transfer to serving glasses and stir in the honey.

Sprinkle with chia seeds and refrigerate for 20 minutes before serving.

Enjoy!

Nutrition information per serving: Kcal: 118, Protein: 8g, Carbs: 20g, Fats: 1.3g

12. Tuna Steaks with Celery

Ingredients:

1 lb of tuna steaks

1 cup of celery, chopped

1 cup of olive oil

2 tbsp of lemon juice, freshly squeezed

1 tbsp of fresh rosemary, finely chopped

1 tsp of dried basil, finely chopped

½ tsp of sea salt

¼ tsp of black pepper, ground

Preparation:

Wash the tuna steaks and pat dry with a kitchen paper. Set aside.

Wash the celery under cold running water and cut into bite-sized pieces. Set aside.

In a large bowl, combine oil, lemon juice, rosemary, basil, salt, and pepper. Soak the tuna in this marinade and wrap the bowl with a plastic foil or a cover with a lid. Refrigerate for at least 1 hour. Coat the meat with marinade occasionally.

Now, use about 2 tablespoons of the marinade and heat it up in a large skillet over a medium-high temperature. Add celery and cook for 5 minutes, or until soften. Remove the celery and reserve the pan. Add steaks and cook for about 3-4 minutes on each side, or until desired doneness. Add more marinade if needed. Remove from the heat and serve immediately.

Enjoy!

Nutrition information per serving: Kcal: 308, Protein: 34.2g, Carbs: 1.5g, Fats: 17.9g

13. Chicken Eggplant Skewers

Ingredients:

1 lb of chicken breasts, skinless, boneless, cut into bite-sized pieces

1 cup of eggplant, cut into bite-sized pieces

2 tbsp of fresh cilantro, finely chopped

1 cup of olive oil

2 tbsp of lemon juice, freshly squeezed

½ tsp of sea salt

¼ tsp of black pepper, ground

¼ tsp of cayenne pepper, ground

Preparation:

Wash the chicken breasts under cold running water and pat dry with a kitchen paper. Cut into bite-sized pieces and set aside.

Wash the eggplant and cut into bite-sized pieces. Set aside.

In a large bowl, combine olive oil, lemon juice, salt, pepper, and cayenne pepper. Mix to blend and then add chicken chops and eggplant. Wrap the top of the bowl with some plastic foil and refrigerate for at least 1 hour.

Preheat the grill to medium-high temperature. If you are using wooden skewers, soak them in water for 10 minutes before using.

Arrange meat and eggplant onto a skewer and place it on a grill. Repeat the process with the remaining ingredients.

Grill for about 8-10 minutes turning occasionally, or until lightly charred. Brush with the remaining marinade to keep it juicy.

Enjoy!

Nutrition information per serving: Kcal: 378, Protein: 44.1g, Carbs: 2g, Fats: 20.7g

14. Red Omelet

Ingredients:

5 large eggs

1 medium-sized tomato, chopped

1 small onion, sliced

1 tbsp of sour cream

1 tbsp of olive oil

1 tsp of dried oregano, ground

¼ tsp of salt

¼ tsp of black pepper, ground

Preparation:

Wash the tomato and cut into quarters. Place it in a blender and season with oregano. Process until smooth and set aside.

Beat the eggs in a large bowl and sprinkle with some salt and pepper. Set aside.

Preheat the oil in a large skillet over a medium-high temperature. Add onions and stir-fry for about 3-4 minutes, or until translucent. Add pureed tomatoes and cook for 1 minute.

Now, add eggs and spread evenly. Cook for 3 minutes and then flip the omelet. Cook for 2 more minutes and remove from the heat. Spread the sour cream and fold the omelet.

Serve immediately.

Nutrition information per serving: Kcal: 308, Protein: 34.2g, Carbs: 1.5g, Fats: 17.9g

15. Turkey with Avocado and Pepper

Ingredients:

1 lb of turkey breasts, cut into bite-sized pieces

1 cup of avocado, cubed

1 large red bell pepper, chopped

1 cup of Iceberg lettuce, shredded

½ cup of cheddar cheese, crumbled

2 tbsp of olive oil

¼ tsp of salt

¼ tsp of black pepper, ground

¼ tsp of cayenne pepper, ground

Preparation:

Wash the meat and pat dry with a kitchen paper. Cut into bite-sized pieces and set aside.

Peel the avocado and cut in half. Remove the pit and cut into cubes. Set aside.

Wash the bell pepper and cut in half. Remove the seeds and chop into thin rings. Set aside.

Preheat the oil in a large skillet over a medium-high temperature. Add pepper and avocado. Cook for 2 minutes and then add meat. Sprinkle with some salt, pepper, and cayenne pepper. Stir well and cook for about 4-5 minutes, stirring occasionally. Remove from the heat.

Spread the shredded lettuce onto a serving plate. Spoon the meat and veggies and top with crumbled cheese. Serve immediately.

Nutrition information per serving: Kcal: 429, Protein: 31.9g, Carbs: 14.6g, Fats: 27.7g

16. Shrimp Zucchini Stew

Ingredients:

1 lb of shrimps, cleaned and deveined

1 large zucchini, thinly sliced

2 cups of vegetable broth

¼ cup of spring onions, chopped

2 tbsp of olive oil

1 tsp of balsamic vinegar

1 tsp of cayenne pepper, ground

1 tsp of rosemary, finely chopped

¼ tsp of sea salt

¼ tsp of black pepper, ground

Preparation:

Clean and devein the shrimps. Rinse well and pat dry with a kitchen paper. Set aside.

Wash the zucchini and cut into thin slices. Set aside.

Preheat the oil in a deep pot over a medium-high temperature. Add onions and zucchini. Cook for 5 minutes, stirring occasionally. Add shrimps and about 2 tablespoons of vegetable broth. Sprinkle with some salt, pepper, and cayenne. Stir well and cook for 3 more minutes.

Now, add the remaining broth and sprinkle with rosemary. Bring it to a boil and reduce the heat to low. Cook for about 6-8 minutes and then remove from the heat.

Serve warm.

Nutrition information per serving: Kcal: 309, Protein: 39.2g, Carbs: 7.9g, Fats: 13.2g

17. Flank Steak with Potatoes

Ingredients:

1 lb of lean flank steak

10 oz of small new potatoes, halved

2 tbsp of olive oil

1 tsp of yellow mustard

1 tbsp of apple cider vinegar

1 tsp of sea salt

½ tsp of black pepper, ground

¼ cup of chives, chopped

1 tsp of fresh parsley, finely chopped

Preparation:

Wash the meat under cold running water and pat dry with a kitchen paper. Set aside.

Peel the potatoes and place them in a pot of boiling water. Add a pinch of salt and cook for 15 minutes, or until fork-tender. Remove from the heat and drain.

Transfer the potatoes to a large bowl, and add chives,

pepper, mustard, and vinegar. Set aside.

Now, preheat the oil in a large skillet over a medium-high temperature. Add steak and sprinkle with salt and parsley. Cook for about 3-4 minutes for medium-rare, or until desired doneness. Remove from the heat and transfer to a cutting board. Let it stand for 5 minutes, then slice into the desired size.

Serve steak with potatoes. Garnish with some lemon slices and enjoy!

Nutrition information per serving: Kcal: 459, Protein: 43.9g, Carbs: 19.5g, Fats: 22.1g

18. Orzo Squash Salad

Ingredients:

1 lb of yellow squash

10 oz of orzo pasta

1 tbsp of olive oil

¼ cup of pine nuts

1 tbsp of lemon juice, freshly squeezed

1 tsp of apple cider vinegar

¼ tsp of salt

¼ tsp of black pepper, ground

1 tbsp of fresh mint, finely chopped

Preparation:

Cook the pasta using package instructions. Drain well and cover with a lid. Set aside to cool for a while.

Wash the squash and cut lengthwise into thin strips, about 1-inch thick. Set aside.

Preheat a dry frying pan over a medium-high temperature. Add pine nuts and fry for 4 minutes, or until browned.

Remove from the heat and set aside.

In a large bowl, combine oil, lemon juice, vinegar, salt, pepper, and mint. Stir well to combine and soak the squash strips into this mixture. Coat well and let it soak for 5 minutes.

Meanwhile, preheat the grill to a medium-high temperature. Grill the squash strips for about 5-8 minutes, or until lightly charred. Remove from the grill and transfer to a large salad bowl.

Add pasta and mix it with grilled squash. Drizzle with the remaining marinade and top with toasted pine nuts.

Serve immediately.

Nutrition information per serving: Kcal: 312, Protein: 10.6g, Carbs: 44g, Fats: 11.2g

19. Cheesy Tomatoes

Ingredients:

4 large tomatoes, whole

½ cup of Feta cheese, crumbled

1 tbsp of olive oil

1 small cucumber, finely chopped

1 tbsp of sour cream

1 tbsp of fresh parsley, finely chopped

¼ of black pepper, ground

Preparation:

Preheat the oven to 375°F.

Wash the cucumber and finely chop it. Set aside.

In a small bowl, combine cheese, sour cream, parsley, garlic, and cucumber. Stir until well incorporated and set aside.

Wash the tomatoes and slice the caps, about ½ inch from the top. Carefully scoop out the tomato flesh.

Grease a large baking sheet with oil.

Now, spoon the cheese mixture into the tomatoes. Spread the tomatoes with 1-inch space between each tomato. Return the caps and close the tomatoes with it. Place it in the oven and bake for about 10-12 minutes, or until tomatoes soften.

Remove from the oven and set aside to cool for a while before serving.

Nutrition information per serving: Kcal: 261, Protein: 9.8g, Carbs: 21.5g, Fats: 17.2g

20. Dried Fruit Porridge

Ingredients:

1 cup of rolled oats

1 cup of almond milk

2 tbsp of raisins, chopped

2 dried figs, chopped

1 tbsp of toasted almonds, roughly chopped

1 tbsp of coconut flour

1 tsp of lemon zest

Preparation:

Combine oats and 1 cup of water in a deep pot. Bring it to a boil and cook for 2 minutes. Remove from the heat and fluff with a fork. Allow it to cool completely. Now, combine oats with almonds milk and stir in the raisins and figs. Stir well and top with coconut flour and lemon zest before serving.

Nutrition information per serving: Kcal: 553, Protein: 10.7g, Carbs: 11.9g, Fats: 34g

21. Chicken with Creamy Snow Peas

Ingredients:

1 lb of chicken fillets, thinly sliced

1 cup of snow peas

2 tbsp of olive oil

1 large egg white

1 tbsp of sour cream

1 tbsp of balsamic vinegar

½ tsp of salt

¼ tsp of black pepper, ground

Preparation:

In a medium bowl, combine egg white, vinegar, sour cream, salt, and pepper. Stir until well incorporated. Set aside.

Preheat the oil in a large frying pan over a medium-high temperature. Add chicken fillets and cook for about 3-5 minutes on each side, or until golden brown. Transfer the meat to a plate and reserve the pan.

Add the previously prepared sauce to the pan and cook until heated through. Add snow peas and cook for 5 minutes, or until nicely tender. Remove from the heat and serve with fillets. Pour the remaining sauce over the fillets. Drizzle with some fresh lemon juice, but this is optional.

Nutrition information per serving: Kcal: 405, Protein: 46.8g, Carbs: 4.2g, Fats: 21.5g

22. Black Bean Tortillas

Ingredients:

1 cup of black beans, pre-cooked

½ cup of corn

1 large red bell pepper, chopped

4 cherry tomatoes, sliced

1 small red onion, sliced

1 tbsp of olive oil

2 tbsp of sour cream

1 tsp of dried oregano, ground

¼ tsp salt

¼ tsp of cayenne pepper, ground

¼ tsp of black pepper, ground

4 large Romaine lettuce leaves

4 buckwheat tortillas

Preparation:

In a medium bowl, combine oil, cream, oregano, salt,

cayenne pepper, and black pepper. Stir well and set aside to allow flavors to blend.

Place the beans in a deep pot. Add 3 cups of water and bring it to a boil. Cook for 15 minutes, or until tender. Add corn and cook for another 5 minutes. Remove from the heat and let it cool for a while.

Wash the pepper and cut lengthwise in half. Remove the seeds and cut into small pieces.

Now, combine cooked beans, corn, and pepper in a medium bowl. Drizzle with previously prepared dressing. Toss to coat well all the ingredients.

Spread the lettuce leaves onto tortillas and spoon the mixture evenly on each. Seal the wrap using a toothpick. Serve immediately.

Nutrition information per serving: Kcal: 355, Protein: 14.9g, Carbs: 61.2g, Fats: 7.1g

23. Chicken Wings with Beans and Tomatoes

Ingredients:

1 lb of chicken wings

1 cup of navy beans

1 cup of cherry tomatoes, halved

2 tbsp of fresh parsley, finely chopped

2 tbsp of all-purpose flour

1 tbsp of olive oil

1 tsp of salt

¼ tsp of black pepper, ground

¼ tsp of chili pepper, ground

2 cups of chicken broth

Preparation:

Place the beans in a pot of boiling water. Cook for 10 minutes and then remove from the heat. Drain well and set aside.

Preheat the oil in a large skillet over a medium-high temperature. Add chicken wings and sprinkle with some salt and pepper. Cook for about 3-4 minutes on each side, or until lightly browned. Pour the broth and bring it to a boil. Add tomatoes and beans. Stir well and reduce the heat. Cook for 5 minutes, stirring occasionally.

Now, combine flour, chili, and 2 tablespoons of water. Stir well until and pour it into the skillet. Cook for another 4 minutes and sprinkle with parsley. Remove from the heat.

Serve warm.

Nutrition information per serving: Kcal: 371, Protein: 38.2g, Carbs: 29.6g, Fats: 10.8g

24. Quinoa Spinach Strawberry Salad

Ingredients:

1 cup of strawberries, sliced

1 cup of fresh spinach, roughly chopped

1 cup of quinoa, pre-cooked

1 tbsp of lemon juice, freshly squeezed

1 tbsp of olive oil

1 tsp of salt

¼ tsp of cayenne pepper

1 tbsp of fresh parsley, finely chopped

Preparation:

In a deep pot, combine quinoa and 2 cups of water. bring it to a boil and then cook for about 13-15 minutes. Remove from the heat and fluff with a fork. Cover with a lid and set aside.

In a small bowl, combine lemon juice, oil, salt, cayenne pepper, and parsley. Stir well and set aside to allow flavors to meld.

Wash the strawberries and cut into thin slices. Set aside.

Wash the spinach thoroughly under cold running water and chop it into small pieces. Set aside.

Now, combine cooked quinoa, strawberries, and spinach in a salad bowl. Stir and then toss with a previously prepared dressing. Toss well to coat all the ingredients and serve immediately.

Enjoy!

Nutrition information per serving: Kcal: 269, Protein: 8.7g, Carbs: 40.7g, Fats: 8.4g

25. Turkey Patties with Tzatziki

Ingredients:

1 lb of ground turkey

1 small red onion, chopped

1 tbsp of fresh dill, chopped

2 garlic cloves, crushed

2 tbsp of fresh parsley, finely chopped

½ tsp of salt

¼ tsp of black pepper, ground

1 cup of Greek yogurt

¼ cup of cucumber, finely chopped

1 tbsp of fresh dill, finely chopped

1 tbsp of lemon juice

1 tsp of honey, raw

1 tbsp of olive oil

Preparation:

In a large bowl, combine ground turkey, onion, dill, garlic, parsley, salt, and pepper. Mix until well incorporated and shape the patties into the desired size.

Preheat the oil in a large skillet over a medium-high temperature. Add patties and fry for about 3-4 minutes on each side. Repeat with the remaining patties until done. Set aside.

Now, you can make tzatziki sauce. In a medium bowl, combine yogurt, chopped cucumber, dill, honey, and lemon juice. Stir well until combined and serve with patties.

You can spread lettuce leaf and spoon the tzatziki onto it, but this is optional.

Enjoy!

Nutrition information per serving: Kcal: 424, Protein: 50.6g, Carbs: 9.4g, Fats: 23.1g

26. Pomegranate Banana Smoothie

Ingredients:

1 cup of pomegranate seeds

1 large banana, chopped

1 cup of Greek yogurt

1 tbsp of lemon juice, freshly squeezed

1 tbsp of honey, raw

1 tbsp of almonds, finely chopped

Preparation:

First, prepare the fruits.

Cut the top of the pomegranate fruit using a sharp knife. Slice down to each of the white membranes inside of the fruit. Pop the seeds into a cup or a bowl and set aside.

Peel the banana cut into chunks. Set aside.

Now, combine pomegranate seeds, banana, yogurt, lemon juice, and honey in a food processor. Blend until nicely smooth and transfer to serving glasses. Top with almonds and refrigerate for 20 minutes before serving.

Enjoy!

Nutrition information per serving: Kcal: 162, Protein: 2g, Carbs: 37g, Fats: 1.8g

27. Carrot Coconut Soup

Ingredients:

6 large carrots, thinly sliced

2 cups of coconut milk

1 medium-sized sweet potato, chopped

1 small onion, chopped

2 cups of chicken broth

1 tsp of curry powder

2 garlic cloves, crushed

1 tbsp of vegetable oil

1 tsp of salt

¼ tsp of black pepper, ground

Preparation:

Preheat the oil in a deep pot over a medium-high temperature. Add onions and stir-fry onions until translucent. Add garlic and mix well with onions. Cook for another minute.

Add carrots, potatoes, and chicken broth. Bring it to a boil and sprinkle with curry, salt, and pepper. Cook for 15 minutes and then add coconut milk. Cook until heated through and remove from the heat.

Transfer the soup to a food processor in a few batches. Return the soup to a pot and reheat it.

Serve warm.

Nutrition information per serving: Kcal: 406, Protein: 7g, Carbs: 26.1g, Fats: 32.8g

28. Grilled Squids and Peppers

Ingredients:

1 lb of small squids

1 cup of extra-virgin olive oil

1 tsp of fresh rosemary, finely chopped

1 large red bell pepper, whole

1 large yellow bell pepper, whole

2 garlic cloves, crushed

½ tsp of salt

¼ tsp of black pepper, ground

1 tbsp of fresh parsley, finely chopped

Preparation:

Wash the squids thoroughly under cold running water. Pat dry with a kitchen paper and set aside.

In a large bowl, combine oil, rosemary, garlic, salt, pepper, and parsley. Soak the squids in this marinade for 30 minutes. Set aside.

Preheat the grill to a medium-high temperature. Add

squids and grill for 5 minutes on each side. Brush the squids occasionally with the remaining marinade. Add the peppers to the grill after 5 minutes. Brush the peppers with the marinade.

Remove the squids and peppers from the grill and serve.

Nutrition information per serving: Kcal: 350, Protein: 35.5g, Carbs: 12.9g, Fats: 16.7g

29. Sun-Dried Tomato Omelet

Ingredients:

5 large eggs, beaten

2 oz of sun-dried tomatoes, finely chopped

1 oz of goat's cheese, crumbled

2 tbsp of skim milk

¼ cup of fresh basil, chopped

1 tbsp of olive oil

½ tsp of salt

¼ tsp of black pepper, ground

Preparation:

In a large bowl, combine eggs, salt, pepper, and milk. Whisk until well incorporated and set aside. Preheat the oil in a large frying pan over a medium-high temperature. Pour in the egg mixture and fry for about 3-4 minutes. Add tomatoes, cheese, and basil in the middle of the omelet and fold.

Remove from the heat and serve immediately.

Nutrition information per serving: Kcal: 302, Protein: 19.7g, Carbs: 3.4g, Fats: 23.8g

30. Cauliflower Kale Stew

Ingredients:

1 cup of cauliflower, chopped

1 cup of fresh kale, chopped

1 medium-sized onion, chopped

1 tsp of cumin, ground

2 medium-sized tomatoes, chopped

2 cups of vegetable broth

½ tsp of turmeric, ground

2 tbsp of fresh parsley, finely chopped

½ tsp of salt

¼ tsp of black pepper, ground

Preparation:

Preheat the oil in a deep pot over a medium-high temperature. Add onions and stir-fry for about 4-5 minutes, or until translucent. Add tomatoes and cook for 3 minutes more, or until soften.

Now, add cauliflower, kale, and vegetable broth. Bring it to a boil and sprinkle with cumin, turmeric, salt, and pepper. Reduce the heat to low and cook for 15 minutes, stirring occasionally. Stir in the parsley and cook for 1 minute more.

Remove from the heat and serve warm.

Nutrition information per serving: Kcal: 140, Protein: 10.5g, Carbs: 22.6g, Fats: 2.1g

31. Coated Chicken with Sweet Potato Puree

Ingredients:

1 lb of chicken breasts, thinly sliced

1 cup of sweet potatoes, chopped

2 tbsp of skim milk

1 tsp of dried thyme, ground

¼ cup of Parmesan cheese, shredded

1 large egg, beaten

1 cup of breadcrumbs

½ tsp salt

¼ tsp of black pepper, ground

1 tbsp of olive oil

Preparation:

Wash the fillets and pat dry with a kitchen paper. Set aside.

Place the sweet potatoes in a pot of boiling water and cook until fork-tender. Remove from the heat and drain. Set aside to cool for a while.

Place the sweet potatoes in a food processor along with

milk and thyme. Process until nicely pureed. Set aside.

Meanwhile, spread the breadcrumbs on a large sheet. Beat the egg, salt, and pepper in a large bowl. Dip the fillets in egg mixture then roll in breadcrumbs. Repeat the process with all meat.

Preheat the oil in a large frying pan over a medium-high temperature. Add the fillets and fry for about 3-5 minutes, or until golden brown.

Serve the fillets with sweet potato puree and sprinkle with Parmesan before serving.

Enjoy!

Nutrition information per serving: Kcal: 617, Protein: 57.8g, Carbs: 41.5g, Fats: 23.6g

32. Blueberry Chia Oatmeal

Ingredients:

1 cup of oatmeal

1 cup of skim milk

¼ cup of blueberries

¼ tsp of cinnamon, ground

1 tbsp of orange juice, freshly squeezed

1 tbsp of honey

1 tbsp of chia seeds

Preparation:

Combine oatmeal and milk in a medium-sized bowl. Stir well and let it soak for 30 minutes. Now, heat it up in the microwave for 2 minutes. Stir in the orange juice, honey, cinnamon, and chia seeds. Top with blueberries before serving and serve immediately.

Nutrition information per serving: Kcal: 266, Protein: 10.4g, Carbs: 47.3g, Fats: 4g

33. Veal Steak with Mushrooms and Spinach

Ingredients:

1 lb of lean veal steak, cut into strips

5 oz of button mushrooms, halved

1 cup of fresh spinach, chopped

¼ cup of spring onions, chopped

2 tbsp of olive oil

½ tsp of salt

¼ tsp of black pepper, ground

½ cup of chicken broth

1 tbsp of balsamic vinegar

1 tsp of ginger, ground

Preparation:

Wash the meat under cold running water and pat dry with a kitchen paper. Cut the steak into thin strips and set aside.

In a small bowl, combine 1 tablespoon of oil, salt, pepper, broth, vinegar, and ginger. Stir well to combine and then soak the meat chops into this marinade. Refrigerate for 20 minutes.

Preheat the remaining oil in a large frying pan over a medium-high temperature. Add meat chops and reserve the marinade. Cook for about 3-5 minutes, or until browned. Stir occasionally. Remove the steak and reserve the pan.

Add mushrooms, spinach, and spring onions. Stir well and cook for 5 minutes, or until greens are wilted. Add the remaining marinade and ½ cup of water. Bring it to a boil and reduce the heat to low. Cook for 3 minutes and then add the meat again. Toss it all to combine and cook for 1 more minute. Remove from the heat and serve.

Nutrition information per serving: Kcal: 429, Protein: 22.6g, Carbs: 17.7g, Fats: 33.2g

34. Broccoli Kale Smoothie

Ingredients:

1 cup of fresh broccoli

1 small cucumber, sliced

1 tbsp of fresh parsley, finely chopped

1 cup of fresh kale, chopped

1 celery stalk, chopped

1 cup of Greek yogurt

½ tsp of ginger, ground

Preparation:

Wash the broccoli thoroughly and cut into florets. Set aside.

Wash the cucumber and cut into thin slices. Set aside.

Combine kale and parsley in a colander and wash under cold running water. Slightly drain and chop into small pieces. Set aside.

Wash the celery and chop it into bite-sized pieces. Set aside.

Now, combine broccoli, cucumber, kale, parsley, celery, yogurt, and ginger. Blend until well creamy and smooth. Transfer to serving glasses and refrigerate for 20 minutes before serving.

Enjoy!

Nutrition information per serving: Kcal: 153, Protein: 16g, Carbs: 17.7g, Fats: 2.9g

35. Grilled Squash Onion Salad

Ingredients:

1 small butternut squash, chopped

½ cup of spring onions, chopped

¼ cup of fresh basil, chopped

¼ cup of cranberries

¼ cup of pecan nuts

3 tbsp of olive oil

2 tbsp of orange juice, freshly squeezed

1 tbsp of lemon juice, freshly squeezed

1 tsp of balsamic vinegar

½ tsp of salt

¼ tsp of black pepper, ground

Preparation:

In a medium bowl, combine orange juice, lemon, vinegar, salt, and pepper, Set aside to allow flavors to meld.

Peel the butternut squash and cut lengthwise in half. Scoop out the seeds and cut into strips. Set aside.

Wash the onions and cut into small pieces. Set aside.

Preheat the grill to a medium-high temperature. Add squash and grill for about 5-7 minutes, turning occasionally. Brush the squash strips with previously prepared marinade. Remove from the grill and transfer to a large salad bowl.

Add onions, basil, cranberries, and pecans. Stir well and drizzle with the remaining marinade.

Serve immediately.

Nutrition information per serving: Kcal: 407, Protein: 4.9g, Carbs: 19g, Fats: 37.5g

36. Trout Cream with Carrots

Ingredients:

1 lb of trout fillets

2 large carrots, peeled

2 tbsp of olive oil

1 tsp of paprika, ground

1 tbsp of lemon juice, freshly squeezed

½ tsp of cumin, ground

½ tsp of salt

¼ tsp of black pepper, ground

Preparation:

Wash the fillets and pat dry with a kitchen paper. Set aside.

In a small bowl, combine paprika, lemon juice, cumin, salt, pepper, and 1 tablespoon of oil. Mix to combine and set aside for 15 minutes to allow flavors to blend.

Preheat the oil in a large frying pan over a medium-high temperature. Add fillets and fry for about 3-5 minutes on each side. Add previously prepared sauce 1 minute before set. You can pour it over or use a kitchen brush and slightly add it to the fillets on both sides. Remove from the heat and let it cool.

Transfer the fillets and liquid from the pan to the food processor. Blend until nicely creamy and pureed.

Wash the carrots and slightly peel them. Cut into 1-inch thick strips and serve with fish cream. You can add bell peppers or some other vegetables on your choice.

Nutrition information per serving: Kcal: 392, Protein: 40.9g, Carbs: 5.5g, Fats: 22.4g

37. Broccoli Penne

Ingredients:

1 lb of fresh broccoli, chopped

8 oz of penne pasta

½ small chili pepper, finely chopped

2 garlic cloves, crushed

2 tbsp of olive oil

2 tbsp of Parmesan cheese, grated

¼ tsp of salt

¼ tsp of black pepper, ground

Preparation:

Wash the broccoli and trim off the outer layers. Chop into bite-sized pieces and set aside.

Preheat the oil in a large frying pan over a medium-high temperature. Add garlic and chili pepper. Stir-fry for 1 minute and then add broccoli. Sprinkle with some salt and pepper. Stir once and reduce the heat to low. Cook for about 8-10 minutes.

Meanwhile, cook the pasta al dente, according to package

instructions. This should take probably around 8 minutes. When done, remove from the heat and drain.

In a large bowl, combine cooked pasta and fried broccoli. Sprinkle with grated cheese and toss well to coat.

Serve immediately.

Nutrition information per serving: Kcal: 398, Protein: 17.4g, Carbs: 52.8g, Fats: 14.6g

38. Broccoli Omelet

Ingredients:

1 cup of fresh broccoli, chopped

5 large eggs, beaten

1 tbsp of fresh parsley, finely chopped

5 green olives, pitted

¼ cup of Parmesan cheese, grated

¼ tsp of black pepper, ground

2 tbsp of skim milk

Preparation:

Pour 3 cups of water in a heavy-bottomed pot. bring it to a boil and add broccoli. Cook for about 5 minutes, or until fork-tender. Remove from the heat and drain well. Set aside.

In a large bowl, whisk the eggs, parsley, olives, cheese, and black pepper. Whisk until well incorporated and set aside.

Now, preheat the oil in a large frying pan over a medium-high temperature. Pour in the egg mixture and cook for 2 minutes. Add broccoli on one half of the omelet and cook for 2 more minutes. The broccoli will stick to the omelet while frying.

Remove from the heat when eggs are done. Fold the omelet and serve immediately.

Nutrition information per serving: Kcal: 263, Protein: 22.3g, Carbs: 6.7g, Fats: 17g

39. Salmon & Veggies

Ingredients:

1 lb of wild salmon fillets, skinless and boneless

1 cup of white rice, long grain

1 cup of chicken broth

1 small zucchini, peeled and sliced

2 small carrots, sliced

1 tbsp of olive oil

¼ cup of lemon juice

1 tsp of fresh rosemary, finely chopped

¼ tsp of black pepper, ground

¼ tsp of sea salt

Preparation:

Preheat the oven to 375°F.

Combine salmon, lemon juice, rosemary, olive oil, salt, and

pepper in a glass bowl. Coat well the meat and refrigerate 30 minutes before grilling.

Combine the rice and chicken broth to a medium pot over a medium-high temperature. Add carrots, zucchini, and sprinkle with some salt and pepper to taste. Bring it to a boil and remove from the heat. Set aside.

Place the salmon fillets in a large baking sheet over a piece of baking paper. Coat the fillets with rice and veggies mixture. Cover with aluminum foil and put it in the oven. Bake for about 10-15 minutes or until set. Serve warm.

Nutrition information per serving: Kcal: 347, Protein: 28.4g, Carbs: 28.3g, Fats: 17.6g

40. Cucumber Mint Smoothie

Ingredients:

1 large cucumber, chopped

1 cup of spinach, pre-cooked

1 tbsp of honey

¼ cup of mint leaves

1 cup of Greek yogurt

1 tbsp of lemon juice

1 tbsp of chia seeds

Preparation:

Place spinach in a pot of boiling water. Cook for 10 minutes or until soften. Drain and set aside to cool completely.

Now, combine spinach and all other ingredients in a blender. Blend until smooth and transfer to a serving glass.

Garnish with some fresh mint leaves and refrigerate for 30 minutes before serving.

Nutrition information per serving: Kcal: 130, Protein: 3.8g, Carbs: 31.6g, Fats: 0.7g

41. Gouda Onion Omelet

Ingredients:

4 free-range egg whites

1 free-range egg

3 tbsp of Gouda cheese, shredded

1 tbsp of skim milk

1 small onion, sliced

2 tsp of grapeseed oil

1 tsp of Dijon mustard

2 tbsp of white quinoa, pre-cooked

Preparation:

Pour one cup of water into a small pot and bring it to a boil. Spoon in the quinoa and cook for 15minutes. Remove from the heat and set aside to cool.

Meanwhile, preheat 1 tablespoon of grapeseed oil in a large saucepan over a medium-low temperature. Add the onion and a 1 tablespoon of water. Cover with a lid and cook until translucent. Remove from the heat and add mustard. Stir well to combine. Set aside.

Preheat another tablespoon of grapeseed oil in a large saucepan over a medium-low temperature. Whisk the egg and egg whites in a mixing bowl. Add milk and pour the mixture into the saucepan. Cook for about 4-5 minutes from both sides. Spread the previously prepared quinoa and onions over one half and fold the omelet.

Sprinkle with shredded Gouda and salt to taste.

Nutrition information per serving: Kcal: 210, Protein: 14.3g, Carbs: 18.5g, Fats: 8.6g

42. Ziti Casserole

Ingredients:

4 oz of ziti pasta

6 oz of ricotta cheese, crumbled

6 oz of cheddar cheese, crumbled

2 medium-sized carrots, sliced

2 medium-sized red onions, finely chopped

1 can of tomato sauce

1 garlic clove, crushed

1 medium-sized bell pepper, chopped

1 medium-sized zucchini, sliced

1 can of cherry tomatoes, halved

1 can of black beans, rinsed and drained

8 oz of frozen corn, thawed

1 tbsp of olive oil

1 tsp of dried oregano, ground

½ tsp of chili pepper, ground

¼ tsp of black pepper, ground

Preparation:

Preheat the oven to 375°F.

Preheat the oil in a large skillet over a medium-high temperature. Add garlic and onions, and stir-fry for 2-3 minutes. Now, add pepper, zucchini, and carrots and stir one again. Cook for another 10 minutes stirring constantly. Pour over the tomato sauce and canned tomatoes. Sprinkle with oregano and stir all well. Cook until boils and reduce the heat to low. Cook for another 15 minutes stirring occasionally. Add beans and corn. Sprinkle with chili pepper and stir again. Cook for 5 minutes more and remove from the heat. Gently stir in the pasta and cheeses. Transfer to a casserole dish. Put it in the oven and bake for 30 minutes. Remove from the oven and set aside for 5 minutes to cool. Serve warm.

Nutrition information per serving: Kcal: 440, Protein: 20.4g, Carbs: 59.3g, Fats: 17.1g

43. Avocado and Beet Salad

Ingredients:

1 medium-sized avocado, peeled and chopped

4 medium-sized beets, peeled and chopped

2 cups of cherry tomatoes, halved

1 medium-sized pear, cored and chopped

1 large carrot, sliced

2 tbsp of cashews, chopped

1 tbsp of olive oil

1 tbsp of balsamic vinegar

¼ tsp of Cayenne pepper, ground

¼ tsp of sea salt

¼ tsp of black pepper, ground

Preparation:

Place the beets in a large pot. Pour enough water to cover

all and bring it to a boil. Cook for 15 minutes or until fork-tender. Remove from the heat and drain. Set aside.

Combine vinegar, oil and cayenne pepper in a small mixing bowl. Whisk well and set aside.

Meanwhile, combine avocado chops, carrot, and cherry tomatoes in a large salad bowl. Add cooked beets and pour over the sauce. Stir all well and sprinkle with cashews, salt and pepper.

Serve immediately.

Nutrition information per serving: Kcal: 202, Protein: 2.7g, Carbs: 16.7g, Fats: 15.5g

44. Rice with Pears

Ingredients:

4 cups of brown rice, pre-cooked

2 large pears, cored and cubed

½ cup of spring onions, finely chopped

½ cup of fresh celery, diced

3 tbsp of vegetable oil

3 tbsp of lemon juice

2 garlic cloves, crushed

¼ tsp of black pepper, ground

¼ tsp of fresh ginger, ground

¼ tsp of salt

Preparation:

Combine garlic, ginger, salt, pepper, and lemon juice in a medium-sized bowl. Stir well and add pear cubes. Coat well and mix. Set aside.

Meanwhile, place rice in a large pot. Pour enough water to cover and bring it to a boil. Add spring onions, celery, and oil. Stir well and cook for until set. Remove from the heat and let it cool. Transfer to a serving bowl and gently stir in the pears mixture. Refrigerate for 20 minutes before serving.

Nutrition information per serving: Kcal: 527, Protein: 9.8g, Carbs: 98.1g, Fats: 10.3g

45. Salmon with Spinach in Dijon Sauce

Ingredients:

1 lb of salmon fillets, skinless and boneless

4 tbsp of Dijon mustard

1 tbsp of olive oil

1 tbsp of honey

1 tsp of dried dill

¼ tsp of salt

¼ tsp of black pepper, freshly ground

1 cup of spinach, chopped

2 garlic clove, minced

Preparation:

Combine honey, dill, mustard, salt, and pepper in a small bowl. Stir well to combine. Place filets in a large bowl and pour over the marinade. Coat the meat with a spoon and set aside for 1 hour.

Place spinach in a pot of boiling water. Cook for 5 minutes and remove from the heat. Drain and set aside.

Preheat the oil in a large frying pan over a medium-high temperature. Add garlic and stir-fry until translucent. Add the meat and reserve the marinade. Cook for about 3-5 minutes on both sides, or until flakes. Transfer the meat to a serving plate, but reserve the pan and reduce the heat to low. Add spinach cook for 10 minutes, stirring constantly. Remove from the heat and add it to the serving plate.

Drizzle with previously used marinade and sprinkle with some extra salt and pepper.

Nutrition information per serving: Kcal: 234, Protein: 23.4g, Carbs: 10.4g, Fats: 13.8g

46. Blackberry Mango Smoothie

Ingredients:

¼ cup of blackberries

1 small mango, cubed

1 large pear, chopped

3 tbsp of walnuts, roughly chopped

1 tbsp of honey

1 tsp of hempseed

1 cup of water

Preparation:

Combine all ingredients in a food processor. Blend until nicely smooth. Transfer to a serving glasses. Garnish with mint leaves and walnuts. Refrigerate for 1 hour before serving.

Nutrition information per serving: Kcal: 253, Protein: 4.8g, Carbs: 47.1g, Fats: 7.7g

47. Cucumber Salad with Tomato Vinaigrette

Ingredients:

2 large cucumbers

2 cups of Iceberg lettuce, chopped

1 small onion, sliced

1 tbsp of sour cream

3 tbsp of white wine vinegar

1 tsp of Worcestershire sauce

½ cup of sun-dried tomatoes, finely chopped

1 garlic clove, minced

1 tsp of parsley, finely chopped

1 tsp of honey

¼ tsp of black pepper, ground

2 tbsp of extra-virgin olive oil

Preparation:

Combine sour cream, Worcestershire sauce, vinegar, sun-dried tomatoes, garlic, honey, oil, pepper, and salt in a jar or a small mixing bowl. Stir well and seal with a lid. Refrigerate overnight to allow flavors to meld.

Combine cucumbers, lettuce, and onions in large salad bowl. Drizzle with marinade and sprinkle with fresh parsley.

Nutrition information per serving: Kcal: 179, Protein: 1.4g, Carbs: 11.2g, Fats: 15.4g

48. Cauliflower and Broccoli Soup

Ingredients:

1 lb of cauliflower, chopped

1 lb of broccoli, halved

5 cups of chicken broth

2 tbsp of olive oil

2 garlic cloves, minced

1 tbsp of Dijon mustard

1 tsp of vegetable seasoning mix

½ tsp of salt

Preparation:

Preheat the oil in a large pot over a medium-high temperature. Add garlic and stir-fry until translucent. Add cauliflower, broccoli, and salt. Pour over the stock and bring it all to a boil. Reduce the heat to low and simmer for 20 minutes, or until fork-tender. Remove from the heat and let it cool for a while.

Transfer to a food processor and blend for 2 minutes, or until nicely smooth. Add mustard and sprinkle with vegetable seasoning mix and re-blend.

Transfer the soup to a pot and cover. Add more chicken broth or water if it is too thick and heat it up again.

Serve warm.

Nutrition information per serving: Kcal: 120, Protein: 7.8g, Carbs: 10.3g, Fats: 6.2g

49. Chicken in Lemon & Rosemary Sauce

Ingredients:

1 chicken, (3-4 lb), whole

3 small potatoes, peeled and wedged

1 cup of lemon juice

1 tsp of dried rosemary

½ tsp of vegetable seasoning mix

¼ tsp of black pepper, ground

¼ tsp of salt

Preparation:

Preheat the grill over a medium-low temperature.

Combine lemon juice, rosemary, vegetable seasoning mix, pepper, and salt in a large baking dish. Stir well to combine. Cut the chicken in half in a put it in the bowl. Coat well the chicken with marinade. Cover and set aside to marinate for 2 hours.

Meanwhile, place potatoes in a pot of boiling water. Cook until fork-tender. Remove from the heat and let it cool. Cut into wedges and transfer to a baking dish with the meat.

Grill the chicken for 1 hour, turning several times until nicely golden brown. Remove from grill.

Garnish with fresh rosemary and serve.

Nutrition information per serving: Kcal: 309, Protein: 50.6g, Carbs: 10.8g, Fats: 5.5g

50. Leek Salad with Walnuts

Ingredients:

8 small leeks, chopped

2 garlic cloves, minced

¼ cup of shallots, minced

¼ cup of walnuts, roughly chopped

1 tsp of yellow mustard

2 tbsp of balsamic vinegar

2 tbsp of olive oil

1 tbsp of chives, minced

1 tsp of fresh parsley, finely chopped

¼ tsp of salt

¼ tsp of black pepper, ground

Preparation:

Combine garlic, shallots, mustard, and walnuts in a small

mixing bowl or a jar. Pour the vinegar and oil. Give it a good stir, or if using a jar, seal the lid. Sprinkle with parsley, chives, salt and pepper. Set aside for 30 minutes to allow flavors to mingle.

Meanwhile, place the leeks in a large saucepan over a medium-high temperature. Pour enough water to cover and bring it to a boil. Reduce the heat to low and cover with a lid. Simmer for about 10-12 minutes more, or until set. Remove from the heat and drain well. Transfer to a salad bowl.

Pour over the marinade over the leeks. Let it cool and refrigerate 10 minutes before serving.

Nutrition information per serving: Kcal: 121, Protein: 2.3g, Carbs: 3.2g, Fats: 11.7g

51. Fish Nuggets with Tomato Sauce

Ingredients:

8 oz of trout fillets, cubed

½ cup of breadcrumbs

1 large egg

2 tbsp of Greek yogurt

¼ cup of skim milk

1 tbsp of lemon juice

¼ tsp of salt

¼ tsp of black pepper, ground

For the sauce:

2 large tomatoes, pureed

1 tbsp of lemon juice

¼ tsp of chili pepper, ground

¼ tsp of dried oregano, ground

Preparation:

Preheat the oven to 375°F.

Combine tomatoes, chili, oregano, and lemon juice in a food processor. Blend until smooth. Set aside.

Beat the egg in a medium-sized bowl. Add yogurt and milk. Sprinkle with some salt and pepper to taste and whisk well to combine.

Now, dip the fish into the egg mixture, then roll in breadcrumbs.

Place some baking paper on a baking sheet. Spread the fish evenly and put it in the oven. Bake until golden brown. Remove from the oven.

Serve baked nuggets with tomato sauce or simply drizzle over.

Nutrition information per serving: Kcal: 204, Protein: 19.8g, Carbs: 14.4g, Fats: 7.1g

52. Mint Strawberry Salad

Ingredients:

2 cups of strawberries, sliced

1 cup of arugula, chopped

½ cup of red cabbage, shredded

½ cup of dates, pitted and chopped

1 cup of Romaine lettuce, chopped

½ cup of sour cream

1 tbsp of fresh mint, ground

2 tbsp of orange juice

¼ tsp of salt

3-4 mint leaves

Preparation:

Combine sour cream, orange juice, ground mint, salt and pepper in a small mixing bowl. Stir well to combine and set aside to allow flavors to mingle.

Combine strawberries, arugula, cabbage, and dates in a large bowl. Stir once, then pour over the previously made sauce.

Garnish with mint leaves and refrigerate for 15 minutes before serving.

Nutrition information per serving: Kcal: 157, Protein: 2.3g, Carbs: 25.5g, Fats: 6.4g

53. Creamy Broccoli

Ingredients:

1 lb of broccoli, chopped

4 oz of cheddar cheese, shredded

3 tsp of cornstarch

1 cup of skim milk

1 tsp of Worcestershire sauce

¼ tsp black pepper, ground

½ tsp of salt

Preparation:

Place the broccoli in a pot of boiling water. Cook until fork-tender and remove from the heat. Drain well and set aside.

Combine cornstarch and milk in a large saucepan over a medium-high temperature. Bring it to a boil and reduce the heat to low. Cook until slightly thickened. Add cheese and sauce. Cook until cheese is melted. Remove from the heat and let it cool for a while.

Transfer broccoli portions into a serving plate. Pour over the sauce and serve.

Nutrition information per serving: Kcal: 185, Protein: 12.3g, Carbs: 13.1g, Fats: 9.8g

54. Turkey Wraps

Ingredients:

12 oz of turkey filets, minced

10 oz of tomatoes, finely chopped

1 small onion, sliced

3 garlic cloves, minced

3 tbsp of tomato sauce

1 tbsp of Worcestershire sauce

1 tsp of paprika, ground

1 tbsp of olive oil

½ tsp of salt

4 lettuce leaves

4 tortillas

Preparation:

Preheat the oil in large pot over a medium-high

temperature. Add onion and garlic and stir-fry until translucent. Add meat, tomatoes, tomato sauce and Worcestershire sauce. Sprinkle with a pinch of salt and stir well. Reduce the heat to low, cover with a lid and cook for 3 hours, or until set. Stir in the paprika and remove from the heat. Let it cool for a while.

Spread one lettuce leaf over the tortilla and spoon the mixture evenly. Wrap and secure with a toothpick.

Nutrition information per serving: Kcal: 259, Protein: 27.5g, Carbs: 17.7g, Fats: 8.7g

55. Spanish Style Chicken

Ingredients:

1 lb of chicken filets, skinless and boneless, chopped

1 cup of chicken broth

2 tbsp of all-purpose flour

2 bell peppers, cut into strips

1 large onion, wedged

2 medium-sized tomatoes, diced

2 tbsp of olive oil

2 garlic cloves, crushed

¼ tsp of Cayenne pepper, ground

¼ tsp of salt

¼ tsp of black pepper, ground

Preparation:

Combine meat chops, flour and salt in a large bowl. Toss

well to combine and set aside.

Nutrition information per serving: Kcal: 303, Protein: 36.1g, Carbs: 14.2g, Fats: 11.2g

ADDITIONAL TITLES FROM THIS AUTHOR

70 Effective Meal Recipes to Prevent and Solve Being Overweight: Burn Fat Fast by Using Proper Dieting and Smart Nutrition

By Joe Correa CSN

48 Acne Solving Meal Recipes: The Fast and Natural Path to Fixing Your Acne Problems in Less Than 10 Days!

By Joe Correa CSN

41 Alzheimer's Preventing Meal Recipes: Reduce or Eliminate Your Alzheimer's Condition in 30 Days or Less!

By Joe Correa CSN

70 Effective Breast Cancer Meal Recipes: Prevent and Fight Breast Cancer with Smart Nutrition and Powerful Foods

By Joe Correa CSN

www.ingramcontent.com/pod-product-compliance
Lightning Source LLC
Chambersburg PA
CBHW052024070526
44584CB00016B/1885